WITNESS

True Events from a Society
Living, Working, and Dying in Trash

By Brett Durbin and
Dr. Jim Congdon

PRESS

Cover and Page Design: Kip Kraisinger, Jon DeMeo
Senior Editor: David Yeazell, dayeazell@juno.com.
Copy Editor: Kris Hallam
Transcription: Carol Mammoliti, Judy Sorensen, Christie Chance, Shelley Setchell

Some names have been changed to protect the identity of children at the request of their parents.

www.xulonpress.com

ACKNOWLEDGEMENTS

JAELLE

Early in the life of the ministry, we had no real idea how things were going to work out, or if this would be something that we would do for just a short season, but we knew that we had to move forward in faith. At first, I think our families thought Trash Mountain Project (TMP) was a nice idea that would probably never actually take off or find stability as a stand-alone organization. But you stood by me and loved me in the midst of the biggest challenge of our lives. You have convinced me that unconditional love between two human beings is possible. I love you more today than ever before. You are the greatest example of Christ as you mother our beautiful children: Gabriel, Matthew, Susan, Josiah, and Jeremiah.

MY FAMILY

You have been an incredible example of generosity and dedication to God's movement, and you were quick to support us in this call. I can honestly say that my family has always been there for me. Even when I was a seriously troubled youth, you did not give up. You never stopped praying, and you never stopped with your support. There is no doubt in my mind that your continued prayer for God's guidance and grace in my life is why I am still here, and why I have been given the opportunity to lead this ministry.

In addition to my wife and parent's love and guidance, my brother Derek has been an inspiration to me and to this ministry. Thank you for continually sharpening me throughout the trials of life. Without you, I don't know where I would be.

JON DEMEO

You have become the best friend and ministry partner God could ever bless me and Trash Mountain with. Thank you for hanging in there and standing in the gap alongside me no matter what.

THE TMP TEAM

For all those who labor to lead the Trash Mountain Project ministry: Josh Bechard, Timm Collins, Jon DeMeo, Jaelle Durbin, Debbie Evans, Gayla Greening, John Kazaklis, Kip Kraisinger, Carol Mammoliti, Chris Mammoliti, Brent Nichols, Shelley Setchell, Isaac Tarwater, Mike Tindell, Ken Vander Hart, and Danny Woods.

MICHAEL BARRETT

Our friendship not only taught me about the true power of a story, but it was also instrumental in the formation of Trash Mountain Project. Thank you for joining us in this life story.

JIM CONGDON

Your friendship and partnership on this book-writing project was instrumental in bringing the biblical stories to life within its pages.

"Miracles are a retelling in small letters of the very same story which is written across the whole world in letters too large for some of us to see." ~ C.S. Lewis

Witness is defined as,
Noun: a person who observes an event
Verb: testify; authenticate
(Source: www.dictionary.com)

TABLE OF CONTENTS

FOREWORD

———————

On a chilly spring morning last year, Brett and I meandered around a wind-blown lake in Topeka, Kansas. As we walked, he began to unfold his heart to me. Brett regaled me with story after story after story of situations which either were grand coincidences, or the fingerprints of divine movements in the life of Brett, the Trash Mountain Project team, and several trash dump communities. He then expressed this question to me: "If I tell people about these stories, in print, or with my voice, do I risk drawing needless attention to myself?"

That Brett had entrusted me with that question, as somewhat of an organizational sustainability mentor, I knew that whatever I said next would either trivialize his concern or harvest it for deeper service in the formation of his missional leader's heart.

"Brett, you did not cause the events that you have been swept up in over the past several years. Obediently, you merely followed God into them. What you saw, you saw as a witness.

In this respect, you show yourself to be in the long line of disciples who had to make sense of the movements of God throughout the ages.

To withhold these eyewitness accounts, to fail to collect the evidence of divine fingerprints, to fail to assemble them so that a jury of concerned citizens can make their own judgments is perhaps to miss the reason why these things have been shown to you.

You are a witness, not the agent of what you have seen.

Have you witnessed these things because God intends to connect your stories to the stories of disciples who work at "ordinary" jobs, navigate family challenges, and try to make sense of how life in their congregations and neighborhoods can extend to the grand story of what God is doing in the 21st century?

What if there exists a contingent of sleeping disciples, bored with the mediocrity of their ordinary circumstances, who need to be awakened to the life-transforming moments of God? And that these stories are what He might use?"

WHERE FAITHFULNESS LEADS

As Brett has discovered, faithfulness to God carries you to a place that resembles the pages of the New Testament. You become alive to extravagant habits of God that confirm old, old truths. "And these signs will accompany those who believe: in my name they will cast out demons; they will speak in new tongues; they will pick up serpents with their hands; and if they drink any deadly poison, it will not hurt them; they will lay their hands on the sick, and they will recover." (Mark 16:17, 18).

You begin to think on such passages, and ask (and know in a new way) what they might have meant. When we do His bidding, we find ourselves in places we never knew existed. This comes from taking the risk of knowing Him deeply and making Him known.

However, you may also find yourself a few steps farther away from the comfortable crowd. You may find yourself decreasingly recognizable to yourself and others. You have entered into the pilgrim journey, and obedience produces in you what it has produced for disciples through the ages: *spiritual loneliness.*

Why did God send angelic and prophetic movements to women—one virginal and another barren—to witness: "that which is conceived in her is from the Holy Spirit" (Matthew 1:20). Or "...when Elizabeth heard the greeting of Mary, the baby leaped in her womb. And Elizabeth was filled with the Holy

Spirit" (Luke 1:41). Does not God know that there are social costs of loneliness to be born when He visits the neighborhood?

ASSIGNED TO BEAR HIS NAME

Those who know the experience I speak of know that *this* loneliness may account for a thousand moments of social awkwardness when they try to explain to others what they are doing with their life.

Being misunderstood is one of the hardest emotional conditions to manage. It is a lonely thing to have deep experiences for which there are too few good words to express well.

But they also know that *this* loneliness has its secrets—friendship with God. In His presence and approval, there is fullness of joy and satisfactions that cause the knower to ask, *"How could I ever be satisfied living any other way?"*

And just as "deep calls to deep" (see Psalm 42:7), so those who have had indescribable experiences seek out one another. To connect our experience and the experience of others is a deep reservoir of friendship with others in God's family.

To the reader: Take these experiences seriously. In them, a humble emerging leader seeks to be faithful with a story that has been given to him, a story that at points defies conventional wisdom and explanation.

And in it, also invites you, the reader, to interrogate your own reality. Could it be that what our friends at Trash Mountain Project have begun to experience in flashes of the spectacular at times and entrustments of rueful suffering at others, is a window into the normal existence expected of all disciples at some level?

Should not we all—if the God revealed in Scripture is your God today—regularly have our breath taken away by what *He* causes us to witness, to face, to engage? We think so.

Whether in neighborhoods lined with Sycamore trees, fire hydrants, recycle bins, and comfortable suburban tract homes, or dirt roads strewn with piles of refuse and unwashed children's faces, God invites us to be *His witnesses* in a world desperate for "repairer[s] of the breach, the restorer of streets to dwell in" (Isaiah 58:12).

May you experience and transcend the lonely experience of being assigned to bear His name taking courage as you seek to restore the streets in the communities into which God has placed you as His witness.

> *"For I will not venture to speak of anything except what Christ has accomplished through me to bring the Gentiles to obedience—by word and deed, by the power of signs and wonders, by the power of the Spirit of God—so that from Jerusalem and all the way around to Illyricum I have fulfilled the ministry of the gospel of Christ..."* (Romans 15:18, 19)

Dr. Russell West
Associate Dean, Beeson Center for Biblical Preaching and Church Leadership
Professor of Leadership Education, Asbury Theological Seminary
Professor of Leadership Development for Mission and Evangelism, Asbury Theological Seminary

INTRODUCTION

Trash Mountain Project started with a prayer and a story that was first told through words and then on film. But the story has changed...and we are no longer using a storyboard or writing the story at all. It is being written right before our eyes by the greatest Storyteller the universe has ever known.

Men have been writing His story for thousands of years, because He came, He conquered, and He rewrote history for all of mankind. His story is the greatest ever told, and it will bring encouragement, hope, and ultimately salvation to all who embrace it...and, more importantly, embrace Him.

You see, the story that follows is not just based on true events; *these are, in fact, true events* that happened to a group of followers of this Great Storyteller. We are writing them down and examining their relevance and meaning because we believe with all that we are that His story is still unfolding. And for us, and for the story that follows, it is unfolding in the most unlikely of places through the most unlikely of people.

We follow in the tradition of many other witnesses. Men and women who took what they heard, what they had seen with their eyes and looked at and touched with their hands—and "what we have seen and heard we proclaim to you also..." (I John 1:3a). And, like John, we desire not to bring glory to ourselves for what we have experienced, but desire that "...you too may have fellowship with us; and indeed our fellowship is with the Father, and with His Son Jesus Christ. These things we write, so that our joy may be made complete" (I John 1:3b-4a).

The dictionary definition of a witness is "a person who observes an event" (noun) or to "testify; authenticate" (verb) something that happened *(Source: www.dictionary.com)*. In a few short years, we have observed much that we are sharing within the pages of this book. We have also learned much about our Father. We testify and authenticate the stories, but also use the stories to point to the greater truths about the heart of God for a lost and suffering world.

WHAT WE HAVE LEARNED

We are called to care for whom and what God cares for: Jesus modeled the heart of the Father for the least, the lost and the forgotten. His ministry touched society's outcasts: Samaritans, women, sinners, and others who were generally overlooked by the secular culture and religious establishment of the day. His grace and power was displayed in a special way in the lives of those who could do nothing to help themselves. It is the same today. God has a special place in His heart for those who are the bottom of the barrel in their societies—the poorest of the poor. And we are called to move beyond our comfort zones and reach out and serve and care for those that God cares for. Henry Blackaby said it well: "Find out where God is at work and join Him there" *(Source: Blackaby, Henry, Experiencing God, B&H Books, 2008).*

God can bring redemption to people in the most despicable situations: Redemption through the power of the cross and resurrection is the core of everything we do. And no person is beyond its power or reach! Christ's sacrificial act set the table for all history. We may feel weak and inadequate to help a dying world, but His power is not weak or limited! If we believe that God never changes, that means His power is more than adequate to do today what He did in Bible times: save, restore, heal, and deliver. And it is in the darkest and most hopeless of circumstances and lives where His redemption appears most powerful. The greater the darkness, His light shines the brightest!

God calls us to obedience: When God calls you to do something, say yes! Your mind may argue the logic of what you are being asked to do. Your family and friends may question the sanity of your supposed obedience. But don't let the obstacles of human logic or circumstances that seem like roadblocks keep you from obedience. My brother Derek said, "Be stupid enough to say yes to God." When God calls, go ahead and think through the logic of your obedience, listen to the conflicting counsel from others, consider the complete insanity of what you are being asked to do, and your complete lack of experience and credentials—and in the end, be stupid enough to say yes!

And as you obey, don't deviate from His path. If He is calling you, He understands the larger picture of what He wants to accomplish through your life. He is the Master Puzzle Maker, who knows how the little pieces you bring to the puzzle fit in with the bigger Kingdom picture. In the midst of walking out your call, you never know, but a seeming small act of obedience may be the key that unlocks something that will affect multitudes of lives for the Lord. Despite trials, difficulties, and dangers, stick with God's plan.

God's provision is present and abundant for His purposes: When you say yes to God and obey His directions, He provides. As you pray for your needs, God works through circumstances and other people to make provision for what He has called you to. There is no such a thing as Kingdom lack, and, when you are obeying the call of the King and working for the Kingdom, His provision will be present. You will need to ask to receive, but when you bring the needs before Him for the thing He has called you to, you can be confident that He will meet those needs. They may not always be met in your timeframe, or through the sources you expect—but He will faithfully provide!

Confidently believe that God will do what He says He will do: God will do what He has promised. Peel back the layers of skepticism from years of secular thinking and abuse and manipulation in the Church. Pray in faith. If God is true, and His Word is true, be bold enough to believe that He has the ability and desire to move in ways that defy human logic to meet human needs.

Those of us in first-world countries often seem to have little need for miracles. We have adequate food, hospitals, medicines, shelter—wonderful safety nets that catch us in our times of need. But there are people who have nothing, who scrounge in the trash dump for a few scraps of metal to pay for their next bowl of rice. They are people without support or help, who often have no other option than God. And God moves on their behalf when they pray. And He moves on our behalf to help meet their needs when we join them in prayer, believing that God is the same yesterday, today and forever!

C.S. Lewis said that "Miracles are a retelling in small letters of the very same story which is written across the whole world in letters too large for some of us to see." We believe God is trying to get our attention. He wants to call us, provide what we need for the call, and send us to care for the least and the lost. In small, humble letters, we've written some of the miracles of guidance, provision, protection, redemption, and healing that we have witnessed.

YOU ARE NOW PART OF THE STORY:

By reading this book, you have officially become part of the story. Not only are you going to share in the story that God has inspired through Trash Mountain Project, but because you purchased this book, kids living in dump communities in the Philippines will receive nutritious food. One hundred percent of any profits from the sale of this book will be used to provide meals for children in the very communities you will be reading about. And this is an ongoing project. We have already begun writing the second book in a series that will report what we witness as God moves throughout the world.

Chapter 1:

PROVIDENCE

———•◦•———

During a trip to the Philippines in late 2012, I witnessed much that had provoked me to prayer and reflection. You see, growing up, I was taught that God no longer did the things I had seen and heard and experienced in that beautiful island nation. Maybe God would occasionally heal someone, but it was very rare today. Maybe He could speak audibly to people today, but we shouldn't expect anything like that in our lives. Maybe He would miraculously protect from evil to the point of sending His angels, but...

I had never seen any of those things when I was growing up in the church. And when I did hear about them, I was quickly told that it was just some heretic or quack that was putting on a fake show to swindle people out of money. I was a skeptic like many others. I had studied so many abuses and false claims in seminary that I came to believe that none of that genuinely existed in our day and time.

But what happens when all that I mentioned above happens to you? What happens when you find yourself in the position of hearing voices and witnessing miracles that cannot be explained by science or simple logic? And what happens when you realize that God had providentially and supernaturally ordered your steps to get you from point A to point B without your conscious awareness of what He was doing?

My drive home from work is usually a relaxing time where I reflect on the events of the day, pray, and begin to turn off everything work-related so that I can be fully mentally and emotionally present with my family. On a typical work day in January of 2013, I left the office, jumped in my car, and began the process of tuning out the day's activities and issues.

As I was in prayer, about five minutes from my home, something flashed in my mind's eye that caught me by surprise. I pulled the car over in a parking lot overlooking Lake Shawnee, a beautiful 83-acre lake in Southeast Topeka, Kansas, and began processing what I had just realized: Did God really reveal His plan for Trash Mountain Project (TMP) and my life early in our call to serve those living in trash dump communities? For the first time, I connected the dots and recognized all that the Lord had done.

POINT A: CAMBODIA

My trip to Cambodia in the summer of 2009 was the major turning point and confirmation for our family to go full time with TMP. But that January day, in 2013, overlooking Lake Shawnee, I was beginning to see that I had missed something. God had seemingly posted a "Go Here" sign right in front of my face during that trip, but I didn't see it.

So much had happened on that journey to Cambodia that one significant message had been overlooked. I mean, who can blame us. On that trip, we were almost murdered, had seen what we now believe were angels, had our enemies see and flee from something we believe were angels, heard an audible voice twice in answer to prayer, took a photograph of a group of people who didn't show up in the photo, and had multiple persons on the other side of the world called by the Lord to prayer, for us, during the exact moment of our distress. In the middle of all that, I missed the main message.

In the midst of all the excitement of that trip, in the car on the way to see the Phnom Penh trash dump community, I had a conversation with our translator Sam. Sam was originally from the Philippines and began to describe the many trash dump communities in his hometown of Manila. He said there had been several dump collapses—a landslide with trash—and many people had died. He mentioned three of the dump areas in Manila: Smokey Mountain, San Mateo, and Payatas. I was very interested in what he was telling me, but needed to take one step at a time. We hadn't even seen the Cambodia dump yet, and we were already committed to serving in some capacity in Honduras.

POINT B: THE PHILIPPINES

The message God was trying to bring to me way back in Cambodia only made sense four years later, driving home from a typical day at work: The Philippines. The place we had witnessed miracle after miracle over the past seven months was already in God's plan way back in the beginning of Trash Mountain Project. When we had decided to visit the Philippines, I knew that it had been a place I had prayed for because of Sam's request years before, but I had missed something.

In Manila, we had no control over which dump communities we were going to visit. A young man, Rick Aranas, had done research for us and set up each of the locations we would see during our first exploratory trip in the Philippines in 2012. Driving around Metro Manila, I didn't recall that Sam had mentioned Manila, nor did I remember him talking about the three specific dump communities.

Three of the four communities Rick chose for us to visit in the Philippines were Smokey Mountain, San Mateo, and Payatas; the very same communities Sam had requested our prayers for. In addition to that crazy "coincidence," there was another fact that sent my mind racing. The last time I had an experience where God literally spoke to me to guide the movement and set the direction for TMP was in Cambodia on that night with Sam. The next time it happened was in Manila, while standing on the San Mateo landfill that Sam had told me about. Wow!

Sitting in my car, overlooking the serene lake a few minutes from my home, I had recognized for the first time that, way back in Cambodia, God had been holding up a huge sign with an arrow pointing toward the Philippines. He had a plan to get us from there to here, opening and closing doors along the way and confirming His direction with all the signs, miracles, and supernatural direction that I once did not believe in. But, you see, that is what the story of Trash Mountain is all about: God's providential move through His grace, power, and love. He has known all along that the story you are about to read would influence the steps we were going take in the coming years.

Chapter 2:

AN UNLIKELY CALL

———◆·◆·◆———

"Behold, I stand at the door and knock..."
(Revelation 3:20)

In 2003, Jaelle and I had been married for just a few months, and I was still struggling through life trying to figure out what I was supposed to be doing. I had begun graduate school working on a Master of Arts in Criminal Justice, with a plan to begin a career in correctional administration. During graduate school, I started to feel that God was calling me to something else—even though I knew I was very far from Him. It seemed like a crazy notion.

As I prayed about it through September and October, I started feeling that if I was going into ministry or doing something full time for God, I really needed to go to seminary. As I prayed over that thought during the fall, I was listening to a tape series on Revelation by Dr. David Jeremiah that my dad had given me.

On Halloween night 2003, Jaelle and I had just left a party and were driving separate cars down a country road towards my parent's house at Lake Sherwood in Topeka. My mom was out of town, so I had borrowed her car, met Jaelle at work, and was doing about 40 to 50 mph, listening to one of the middle tapes in the 64-tape series and praying.

All of a sudden, out of nowhere, a deer leapt out of the woods. Startled, my focus was jerked from the Revelation tape and prayer over to the passenger side of the car—just in time to see the deer smash into the car. Slamming on the brakes, my whole body cramped up as I flung open the door and fell out on the cold hard pavement.

Looking back, I saw that Jaelle had hurriedly gotten out of her car and was on her way to assist me. And the deer that should have been dead because of the impact with my mom's car was standing in the middle of the road, staring at me. And then it ran off into the woods. Jaelle said it appeared like the deer's head had completely spun around and looked back at her. She thought it would have been dead as well. We didn't think much of it—other than the impact had really messed up my mother's beautiful car, and I would probably have to pay for it.

I brushed myself off, and we got back in our cars and finished the trip to my parent's house. Handing out some candy to a few trick-or-treaters, we had a few laughs about the events of the night—except that I was going to have to call my mother and tell her that her car had just been wrecked! And that this time it actually wasn't my fault...let's just say I had a few self-inflicted car destructions throughout my teenage years. After the trick-or-treating died down, we turned out the lights, locked the doors, and went home to our apartment and went to bed. The next morning, Jaelle got up to go to work, while I stayed in bed a little longer before heading off to class.

I woke up to a strange feeling. The air in the room felt different—charged. Then, within minutes of opening my eyes, all of the issues that I had been praying about the months prior—ministry and God's purposes for me—came flooding over me. Overwhelmed by the weight of what I was considering, I jumped out of bed, hit my knees and began to cry. As I poured out my heart to the Lord, I broke out in a sweat. And for the first time in my life—I had never had an experience like that before—God spoke to me clearly. He said, "You missed something." It really caught me off guard, shooting the hair on my neck straight up. Honestly, I was scared.

I sat there on the bedroom floor for a few minutes trying to regain my composure, wiping some of the sweat off my face. As I thought about what I had heard, it dawned on me that I had missed something with the car. So, in my boxers and slippers, I traipsed out to the car and walked around it a couple of times. I couldn't see anything out of the ordinary except for the severely damaged door. Pressed for time and needing to get ready to go to class, I felt confused by everything that had just transpired. What had I missed? Was I just crazy and hearing voices?

Before going back in the house, I sat down in the driver's seat and decided to start the car. Turning the key in the ignition, the radio started blaring, which jerked my memory back to the tape I was listening to when the deer hit the car. I reached over and pushed play on the cassette player. The very first words on the tape, right where it had stopped because of the jolt from the deer, in David Jeremiah's unmistakable voice, was, "I stand at the door and knock" (Revelation 3:20).

At that moment I realized something. The deer hit the passenger side door, literally caving it in. It really didn't affect the rest of the car, it had just knocked in the door. As I processed what had just happened, it was clear to me that it was weird, but wasn't just a coincidence. The fact that that 64-tape cassette series would stop at "I stand at the door and knock" the moment a deer had jumped headfirst into the door of my car...I had never been in an accident with a deer before. The odds of all those things happening at the same time, and coinciding with one another, was too much for me to say it was just a coincidence. Someone was trying to get my attention. He was dealing with me, knocking at my door. The question was if I would obey and walk through the doors He opened?

YOU WANT TO DO WHAT?

Later in the day, I explained to Jaelle that I had been intensely praying for a couple months about going into full-time ministry and attending seminary. I felt that the incident with the deer and the prayers and everything surrounding it was an answer to my prayer for direction. And without Jaelle saying a word, I knew what she was thinking—*you're still struggling with alcoholism, and trying to straighten up your life, our marriage is struggling because of your drinking and dishonesty, and you think Jesus is calling you to full-time ministry?*

It wasn't just Jaelle. The decision didn't make sense to anybody in my life. As I started talking to others about the idea of going to seminary in preparation for ministry, people thought I was crazy and that that idea would soon pass. I couldn't blame them, either, because I wouldn't have backed me up if I was in their shoes.

I went and talked to my pastor, Ed Rotz, about my decision. He was the only one who told me if that was God and I had a real experience with Him, I needed to pay attention. And, of course, he would back me up on whatever I decided. Sometime later, Ed said he was actually very nervous about my decision, but he felt he needed to be supportive if that was what I felt I was supposed to do. And if what I heard and experienced was a message from God, then I needed to follow it. He wasn't about to stand in the way.

After a couple of months of discussion, Jaelle warmed up to the idea, and we decided to start looking at potential schools. Jaelle was interested in pursuing a Master's in Counseling at the time, so we wanted a school with a good counseling program for her and a Master of Divinity program for me. Choice one on our list was Denver Seminary which didn't fit what we were seeking. Once choice one was no longer an option, we made a trip to visit option two: Asbury Theological Seminary. We went on separate tours with our respective programs. Meeting back together over lunch, we looked at each other and knew that this was where we were supposed to be—in Wilmore, Kentucky, of all places. That was a long way from our home in Topeka, Kansas.

So there I was, making the decision to go to seminary with my personal life out of order. The week prior to our Asbury visit, I was still struggling with my drinking, and our marriage was suffering. But God was working—actually calling both of us to turn back to Him as a couple. In early 2004, we visited Fairlawn Heights Wesleyan Church in Topeka, Kansas. A retired NBA player named Bay Forrest was speaking at our church, and his message changed us both mentally and spiritually.

Bay gave an illustration that has stuck with both of us to this day, and actually played a huge role in us deciding to turn our lives completely over to Christ. It was a tale about how certain hunters in Africa catch monkeys. It can be very difficult to corral these intelligent creatures, so hunters have used a more inventive method—trapping a monkey by enticing him. A small jar filled with nuts or other items is placed at the base of a tree, which ultimately attracts the monkey's curiosity.

The opening of the jar allows the monkey to place his hand in, but when he tries to withdraw it, he is unable to do so without letting go of the contents of the jar. Believe it or not, some monkeys will stay there with their hand in the jar until the hunter returns! They are trapped because they are unwilling to let go of something they are holding onto even though it is working against them.

It's not just monkeys who get trapped by what they are unwilling to release. While most of us would not be tempted by peanuts or sweets in a jar, it's amazing the things we will hang onto rather than release them so we can move forward in life. In our case, it was holding on to the material things of the world when Jesus was asking us to give it all to Him. We both knew that God was telling us that night that we needed to get back in line with Him.

We went home and had a real "Come to Jesus" moment together. It wasn't easy. At the time, I was on steroids, striving to be physically bigger and stronger. I had several bottles that I retrieved and broke open into the sink—pouring everything out in front of Jaelle. It was a step of telling God and my wife that I was fully leaving part of the lifestyle that had been so destructive to me and to the lives of those who loved me. We talked well into the night about many other things that we were both struggling with and committed to be honest with each other and walk away from the life of drinking and partying that had consumed us both for so many years.

From that night forward, we started moving in the direction of our call to full-time ministry. Over the next year, I finished my Masters in Criminal Justice, and we had made the decision to move to Kentucky and attend Asbury in the summer of 2005. Before heading off to seminary, Jaelle and I had a trip scheduled to go down to Florida to visit her family and have a little break between graduation and the start of a new program of study. We could never have known the path that this simple vacation would put us on.

A DIVINE APPOINTMENT

Right before our Florida trip, I made a huge mistake. I had not been drinking for some time, but succumbed to temptation and got really drunk at a local bar. I don't know if it was the struggle I was having with self-doubt or the doubt that others had expressed in whether I could truly follow God into full-time ministry, but I screwed up royally that day.

Jaelle could tell what had happened as she had been calling and couldn't get ahold of me. She walked into the bar and found me really drunk, playing one of those horribly inappropriate poker machines, with really risqué pictures of girls on the digital playing cards. It was a real disaster for her to see her husband in that position...you know, her husband who had recently committed to attend Asbury Theological Seminary to answer a call to full-time ministry.

After sobering up a bit, I went to my church and broke down to Pastor Ed, his wife Sharon, my mentor and boss Steve Pearson, and a couple of others. Ed had really stepped out on a limb and backed me on my plans for Asbury and ministry, and this monumental mistake had pushed him over the edge. He had put up with all of my problems and foolishness for so many years. And what I had just done was the final straw. He snapped, "This is total crap! What the hell is wrong with you? Do you realize what you have done?"

It was one of those moments in life where something significant clicked inside me. I knew I had really screwed up. And Ed even made the statement that he wouldn't be surprised if Jaelle left me, and he wouldn't blame her. To hear that coming from the lips of my pastor, my mentor and spiritual father, someone I couldn't have more respect for in this world, a man second only to my own father—it completely crushed me. Not to mention that I made him so mad that he cussed. Before that night, I could never have even pictured him cussing. He didn't talk that way out of His love and dedication to Christ, and I had pushed him to it that night.

I went home and apologized to Jaelle, asking her to hang in there with me, and I promised that I wouldn't do it again. Even though I had repeatedly wounded her and damaged trust in our relationship many times, she didn't walk out on me. After that night, there was never a time when I was drunk again. There were a couple of times in the coming year when I foolishly did drink, but not to the point of excess. However, from just a few months after my first son, Gabriel, was born, I never again tasted alcohol, and never will.

I say all this because it was the lead-in to Jaelle and I going to Florida on vacation. My screw-up put a dark cloud over the trip, but it also gave us a chance to talk and work through what had happened, as I was trying to build up her trust in me once again. While in Florida, we stayed at her uncle and aunt's vacation home. Her grandparents were there, and we had a great time with her family.

The morning we were planning to leave for the airport to return home, we thought the flight we were taking back to

Kansas City was an hour later than it actually was. It was strange, because Jaelle and I and her grandparents all had the itinerary, and we all thought it was an hour later. We got to the airport and learned that the flight that had just pulled away from the gate was ours. But, there was another flight in about an hour. There were two seats left, but they were not together.

We took the tickets, got on the later flight, and the flight attendant informed us that one of the passengers needed to move to sit with their family, which, in turn, put Jaelle and I in seats next to each other. I was in the middle seat and Jaelle was at the window, and there was a guy in the aisle seat.

As we sat down, Jaelle leaned over to me and said she recognized the guy in the aisle seat. She thought she had seen him somewhere before. I didn't recognize him. And then it hit her that he was a pastor with a television ministry. I still didn't recognize him, but she was convinced of who he was. As we got up in the air, we all—Jaelle, me, and the guy in the aisle seat—pulled out our Bibles. We each were doing some type of Bible study, just nerding out next to each other.

At one point, I looked over at the guy and said, "Hello. Hey, are you a pastor or something? Are you preparing a message?" (That's what it looked like he was doing.)

He replied, "Yeah, my name is Jay, and I am the pastor at a church in Lakeland, Florida, and I'm preparing my message for Sunday."

And he asked us what we did.

I responded, "We are actually going to begin attending Asbury Theological Seminary at the end of the summer, and we were down seeing family before moving to Kentucky next month."

We continued to talk the rest of the trip.

At the end of the flight I remember him saying something very interesting that I had never heard before. He said our meeting was a divine appointment. Being unfamiliar with that term, I thought, *ok, whatever that means.* We got off the plane, and, once inside the airport, he gave us both a hug. I looked at Jaelle, and said, "Huh?"

It was a very encouraging time. He was a very encouraging person. And we needed the reassurance God provided through that man at that time in our lives. It seemed that maybe it was a divine appointment as he put it. We exchanged contact information, and he promised to send us a couple of his books.

We later found out he preached on national television. Recognizing he was a busy guy, we didn't want to bug him, so we limited our contact to praying for him and sending him a letter of encouragement from time to time through e-mail.

We started seminary, and very quickly felt that God was leading us to begin our family. Within a few short days, Jaelle was pregnant with our first son. We really enjoyed our seminary experience, and believed that it was our time in the desert to grow closer to Christ and learn about what He had planned for us. At the end of our first year in school, I thought, *I need to send Jay a letter and support him* because we had been watching him on TV and wanted to thank him for all that he does. And that was it. There was no other motive. We just wanted to let him know we were praying for him.

Shortly after that, I received a phone call from Jay. He shared an interesting story with me. God had really laid us on his heart. He admitted that he hadn't thought of us for some time, but that morning he had been thinking and praying for us. Then his assistant brought in his daily mail, which included our letter. He opened it and read it, and it was one of those "pay attention to this" moments. So he picked up his phone and gave us a call. He asked if we were coming down to Florida any time soon for vacation or a family visit. And it just so happened that that coming summer we were going to be driving down from Kentucky for a break at Jaelle's uncle and aunt's vacation home again.

LAKELAND IS CALLING

Leading up to our summer trip to Florida, we had a couple of strange things happen. Jaelle and I had been reading Pastor Jay's book on the *Prayer of Jabez*, and we both were praying the prayer. It's an incredible prayer that God would do something so big in our life that we would have no explanation for it coming to pass outside of Him.

We were sincerely praying that prayer, and I felt a strong confirmation that we were supposed to be connected to Jay's church. Mind you, I had never even been to a Southern Baptist church, let alone ever thought of working or volunteering at one. It was a mega-church, and I was a "nobody" finishing up my seminary training without much of a ministry resume.

Just like with any career, it is one thing to receive an education, but it is a completely different thing to have experience in something. It seemed to be the running joke in seminary that it was nearly impossible to get any ministry experience while being a full-time student. Not only was time a problem with the heavy study load, but when you are in a town just a hair bigger than the high school I graduated from, it is hard to find any good internship opportunities. So, I felt grossly underqualified to work at a mega-church.

One day I went to the prayer room at Asbury, one of my favorite spots on campus. I spent the whole morning praying about this nudge that Jaelle and I were feeling about the church in Florida. I grew very frustrated while praying. It was one of those times where you tell God: I need an answer. Is this of You? Are we supposed to be going to Florida? Are we supposed to be offering ourselves to this church? It just seems crazy. I have little or no experience in ministry. We're not even done with seminary, and this is a mega-church. I was thinking in logical terms, *I am not qualified—I am definitely not qualified to work at this church.* So my final words to the Lord were that I was frustrated and that He needed to say or show me, "Florida" at some point that day. It's never really a good idea to challenge God, but that's what I did. In Christianese we call this, "putting out a fleece."

GOOD WORD: DON'T TRY THIS AT HOME ~ DR. JIM CONGDON

A fleece is the woolen coat of a sheep right after being sheared. The term "putting out a fleece" developed from the story of Gideon who was seeking direction from the Lord about an upcoming battle. One night, he put out a woolen fleece asking God to cover it with dew while the ground around would be dry. The second night he asked God to keep the fleece dry while the surrounding ground would be wet. The Lord answered both his requests, confirming his course of action. Like Gideon, Brett was asking God for a sign to confirm his next course of action—putting out a fleece.

The Bible treats "putting out a fleece" as an evidence of immature faith, not strong faith. Gideon twice put out a fleece because he lacked faith in God's promises to him (Judges 6). But God loves little children, especially little children in the faith, and sometimes gives them special signs He does not give His grown-up children. And God's special favor is evident on Trash Mountain Project even before its founding!

I left the prayer room and went to help a new student and his family move into their house. I was the first member of the moving team to arrive. As I pulled up to the house, this guy comes up and says, "Hey, thanks so much for helping me out. We are excited to be here and we just pulled in from Florida this morning."

I looked at him and started laughing.

With a puzzled look on his face, he asked, "What?"

I quickly replied, "Aw, nothing man!"

It had just clicked that he had said Florida within minutes after I had asked God to tell me Florida. It was a "smile in my head" moment.

And, if that wasn't enough, as I was driving home after helping my new friend from Florida, I looked over at Asbury College, which is directly across the street from Asbury Seminary. There was a huge banner in front of the campus on the lawn. There was some camp coming to visit campus, and the sign said, it was the Florida...something...something...group. It was there in HUGE print—**FLORIDA**. So within a two-hour period of praying, *say or show me Florida*, there I was in Wilmore, Kentucky, and I not only saw it, I heard it. I went home and told Jaelle that this was enough confirmation for us to at least meet with Pastor Jay and explore any options with him.

Prior to our trip, we confirmed with Jay that we were going to have dinner with him and his wife, and then go to his church on Sunday. So the last couple of days that we were in Florida, we went to Lakeland. The church put us up in a really nice hotel on Saturday night, and we were going to have dinner at a great restaurant. And we were thinking, *Wow, they are really being awfully nice to us, just to come visit their church. Are they wining and dining us?* At dinner, we were both nervous until we met Jay and Angie. We relaxed as they were such a nice couple and made us both feel so welcome in this town we had never heard of prior to meeting Jay.

Part of the way through the dinner, I finally got up the guts and said, "I need to say something to you, and it may sound crazy, but I'm going to say it anyway because I think I am supposed to. I don't know in what capacity or what this means, but I feel like God is asking us to offer ourselves in service to your church in some way. And again, I don't know what that means, or in what capacity."

Jay turned to his wife and started laughing. And I was thinking *this is not really the response I was looking for*!

But he quickly replied, "No, no, no!" (It seemed he could tell from our faces of embarrassment that we had taken his reaction the wrong way.) "Let me explain something."

Angie almost looked a little spooked, like she had seen a ghost or something.

He looked at her and said, "What did I tell you when we pulled up into the parking lot tonight?"

She just shook her head and said, "You told me exactly what he just said."

Jay went on to explain that he had told Angie that he was having the same feeling about us, but if it was of God, that we would say exactly what we said to them at that moment. (Literally verbatim, it sounded like.) So we all sat there, kind of dumbfounded at what had transpired.

The next day we attended a worship service and met some of the church staff. From our first impressions, it seemed like a great church. We had honestly never been in a church that size other than a huge one in Lexington, Kentucky, that we affectionately called the "mother ship." We were a bit awed by the whole experience. We were excited, but still very hesitant to get too far ahead of ourselves. We talked about the possibility of working at that church for pretty much the entire 13-hour drive home to Kentucky.

Jay called a couple of weeks later and asked me to pray about a few areas of ministry that I could potentially lead: college and singles ministry, missions, small group pastor, church planting, or discipleship. He then said he would call me in a week to see if we were on the same page about which area was God's will. I felt like we already had a lot of God confirmation about working for that church, but Jay had taken it to another level. I got off the phone with him and instantly started praying about it. I felt my call was to the college and singles ministry, even though I had never once considered that area of ministry. I recognized the decision was not mine—it must be God leading me.

Jay called me back the next week. After opening greetings, I said, "Hey, I got it, at least on my end, but we'll see where you're at."

And he said, "Oh, no, I know what you are going to say. You are going to say college and singles ministry, right?"

I almost dropped the phone, looked over at Jaelle who was in the room with me, and said, "Wow, that would be the one!"

And he said, "We're going to have to find a time when you can come meet with our executive pastor Tim, so we'll be in touch with you and go from there. But this is of God, and we are going to make this thing happen, so just plan that you are going to come on staff with us at some point working in that area of ministry." We didn't know the details of what that meant, which was beyond nerve-wracking and, at the same time, exciting. We felt that our small family was about to embark on a new adventure together. And, were we right.

NERVOUS WAITING

It was our third semester at seminary, and I was getting close to being done with my degree. I had switched from a Master of Divinity to Master of Arts in Christian Leadership. It was a bit of a shift from my original plan, but, since I already had a graduate degree in criminal justice, taking another 96 credit hours in grad school was overkill. But, looking back now, the Christian Leadership program was the best and most appropriate for what I am doing today as it focused on such courses as organizational and cross-cultural leadership. Additionally, I had two specific professors who began to take me under their wing and mentor me, Russell West and Rick Gray. It's great to know that God was in that decision, even though I didn't realize it was Him at the time—I thought the degree change was just my preference. I was still a bit naïve at that point, actually believing that I had some control over how God would decide to use me within His kingdom.

A few months had passed since our dinner with Jay in Florida, and we hadn't gotten much information from the church, not even a phone call. I didn't know that Jay had fallen off a stage while preaching and had been badly hurt. His injury had slowed the process up, and the delays made us nervous. And so we made a decision that was probably a little ahead of the game—we put our house on the market. We wanted to test the market and see if it would be difficult to sell. We knew that we would have to sell the house anyway when we finished seminary, and figured this was just another way that we could express our faith in God that we were "all-in" with this ministry appointment.

When we finally got in touch with Tim Parcheta, the executive pastor, he invited me to come down for an initial interview. So, in early 2007, I traveled to Lakeland and met with Tim. Tim is an intense man, and he put me through the ring of fire—the equivalent of a theological and psychological prostate exam. I also met with the man who would eventually be my boss, Jerry Goodell, met all the staff pastors, and went out to lunch with Jay. Everything seemed to be going well, and I grew even more confident that this was where God would be moving our family.

I returned home feeling elated about the interview, and because there was forward motion after a long delay. But then, we didn't hear anything for several more weeks. The forward motion ground to a screeching halt, and that started to scare us. Our house was on the market. And we had decided not to start classes in the coming spring semester except for one online course. We were counting on moving to Florida to start the new job.

Years later, Tim—"Mr. Intensity"—confided that he intentionally delayed calling me to see how I would respond to the pressure. He wanted to see whether I would allow the system to work, and put my trust in God and the church. Really?! I grew to love that guy.

We finally received an invitation at the beginning of February 2007 to fly down and meet with the hiring committee—the last phase of approval before they brought me on staff. The evening after the final interview, as we were waiting to hear from Jay about the job, we met the progressive worship pastor, Bill Horn, who ended up becoming one of my closest friends later down the road. I worked with him in Lakeland, and ironically he now lives in Topeka, Kansas, and is a pastor at one of our ministry's biggest partners, Fellowship Bible Church. As I was talking with Bill in the movie theater where they housed the college ministry, I received a phone call. It was Jay, and he said, "Congratulations, pack your bags and move to Lakeland!"

After the months of delays, those words took a big load off our backs. We returned to our hotel overjoyed and thanked God together in prayer. The next morning, still in Florida and literally just hours after getting the job, we got a call from our realtor. We had not had a single bite on our house, even though we had it on the market for a few months. We were worried that we wouldn't be able to move because of our house. Our realtor said that a couple had made a solid offer. We countered, they countered, and we sold the house that day.

After months of delays, everything changed in a matter of hours. We returned home, packed up, moved to Florida in late February, and I immediately became the college and young adult pastor at First Baptist Church at the Mall. We were now Floridians!

Chapter 3:

THE DEAF CAN HEAR

———◆———

"Count it all joy, my brothers, when you meet trials of various kinds, for you know that the testing of your faith produces steadfastness." (James 1:2, 3)

"But be doers of the word, and not hearers only, deceiving yourselves. For if anyone is a hearer of the word and not a doer, he is like a man who looks intently at his natural face in a mirror. For he looks at himself and goes away and at once forgets what he was like. But the one who looks into the perfect law, the law of liberty, and perseveres, being no hearer who forgets but a doer who acts, he will be blessed in his doing. If anyone thinks he is religious and does not bridle his tongue but deceives his heart, this person's religion is worthless. Religion that is pure and undefiled before God, the Father, is this: to visit orphans and widows in their affliction, and to keep oneself unstained from the world." (James 1:22-27)

I joined the staff at Church at the Mall optimistically and probably a little naïvely. Even though I was wet behind the ears and hadn't done a whole lot of church work of any kind in my past, I hit the ground running. The very first thing I did was to launch the college and young adult ministry: Converge—focused on loving God and people. I also went into my new role wanting to teach. I had binders and computer files full of skills I had learned in seminary, and I wanted to apply them in real life.

I had really grown to love the Book of James, and decided to teach an eight-week study on the book. It seemed very applicable to our young adults and demonstrated how to live out our faith. James chapter one challenges followers of Christ to evaluate what following Him really means. What does it mean to "Count it all joy...when you meet trials of various kinds..." (James 1:1). Did I have this attitude?

Teachers can attest to the reality that when you are teaching something, God is teaching you more than your students are learning. The James study caused me to ask if I was actually living out my personal faith. Was I facing true trials? Was I serving widows and orphans? Was I without doubt? Honestly, my answers to those questions were a big concern. Little did I know that God was simply preparing my heart and mind for the greatest season of trials that my wife and I had ever faced, and the first domino was about to fall.

GOOD WORD: PURE JOY
~ DR. JIM CONGDON

One of the most profitable devotions you can have is to do what Brett did—read James 1:2-4, and think about its application to your life. You may even want to memorize it, so that you can "pull it out" from your mind when needed. As you ponder these famous words, remind yourself of the following exegetical points:

"Brothers" lets us know that the promise of this passage is not for everyone, but for those who have joined the family of God through faith in Jesus. James uses this title for Christians no less than 15 times! Use it yourself.

"Various trials" occur in our lives. How will we face them? How should we respond? James drops a startling challenge on us: to count them as joy. And not reluctantly as a "kind of" joy, or a partial joy. Rather, we should think of them as "pure joy." This is radical, unnatural behavior. After all, we usually respond to troubles with moaning or whining.

But why? Why should we regard our hard times as pure joy? Answer. Because these trials are really to our advantage! For God, who is working all things for our good (Romans 8:28), is not interested in making our life easy; he's interested in making us strong, and making us like his son. "Testing" refers to the refining process that puts gold in the furnace to cleanse it from impurities. Like gold, our faith needs a refining process to make it pure and strong.

But we must "let patience have its perfect work," which means we must not abort the Lord's work of making us better. Too often, we are so eager to escape our difficulties that we seek any door of escape from the trial. But if we will submit to God and see our trials through to the end, then we will discover that God has improved us, and we will come out of the tunnel complete and intact, more like Jesus than ever. And that's the kind of person each of us was designed to be.

THE TRIAL BEGINS

When I started my new position, we spent several months renovating an old movie theater on the back of the church and made it a space devoted solely to the young adult ministry. As the ministry expanded, my wife was hired to be my administrative assistant—which, hindsight being 20/20, was really not the greatest decision.

Mostly, the reason why this was not a good choice was my fault. Those who know me know that my biggest weakness as a leader is internal communication with staff. Thank God that today I have an amazing team that has allowed me to focus on my strengths and helps shoulder the load of all the details that are sometimes absent from my ADD mind.

Some married couples can work really well together in ministry, but with my gifts and lack thereof, and working in a fast-paced church environment, we did not handle it well. It got to the point that we couldn't turn work off at home, and our entire life was centered on the ministry we were leading. Added to the mix, Jaelle got pregnant with Matthew, our second son, during her time in my employ. The situation became very unhealthy and unbalanced. But, just as with many families in ministry, we needed the income, and had no other choice.

Throughout that first year on the job, I started noticing things in the church that I struggled with but was forced to shrug off. Being young and new to the church, I always wanted to be respectful to my elders and leaders who had been placed in positions over me. But that year I found myself constantly disagreeing with so many of the things we were supposed to focus on as pastors at the church. I had grown weary of why I was even there. You top all of my frustration with the question I was asking myself—what it really looked like to follow Christ—and the perfect storm was forming.

LEANING ON GOD

Jaelle and I were already struggling financially, but due to a strained church budget, we ended up having to take a pay cut. This was really hard for me to deal with as a husband and father. So to help make up for our financial shortfall, I began teaching as an adjunct professor at Southeastern University in Lakeland on the side. Receiving that part-time position was a huge blessing and came just at the right time, but it also added 10 more hours to my already overloaded 60-hour work week.

Jaelle and I were beginning to unravel, and we knew we couldn't turn to the church, as they were unable to help us out with this struggle. We had started a food pantry for the young adult ministry. The economy was dropping in Florida, and many of our people were struggling. Even with three jobs, Jaelle and I had to get food from that food bank. In addition, we received free baby formula from the Compassion House Ministry that our church had in place for homeless outreach.

Around that same time, Jaelle was laid off by the church—along with about a third of the staff for budgetary reasons. All of this happened at the same time: a pay cut for me, and Jaelle lost her job. We were having the most difficult financial struggle of our lives.

Both Jaelle and I were born with a silver spoon in our mouths. We came from upper-middle-class families and had never once worried about where our next meal would come from. All we had ever worried about was what we wanted, not what we actually needed. Sad, isn't it? We were two spoiled kids learning a very valuable lesson from our Father.

Throughout that process, we really started leaning on God and questioning, *are we in the right place? Are we supposed to be at this church? It seemed like a dream job. The way we got here was obviously You. How could this be going so wrong? What part of it is our fault?* I was no perfect pastor and found myself wondering, *am I doing something wrong?* The discomfort of what originally seemed like the dream ministry position caused me to seek God afresh for what it was we were supposed to be doing with our life in ministry.

During this time of personal questioning, I started a prayer ministry with the young adult group at the church. I wanted them to focus on prayer and reaching the least: serving the poor in local and global missions. There was a genuine interest developing among the group to go on a mission trip, so we started praying about where we should go. As we prayed, Latin America was really on my heart and seemed like the logical place. So I began looking for opportunities to take a team to Latin America.

JUST A MISSION TRIP

One Sunday morning as I was walking through the church, a gentleman by the name of Jerry Haag, President of the Florida Baptist Children's Homes (a foster care, children's outreach ministry throughout Florida that at the time was starting international child care), stopped me in the hall.

He said, "Hey, you know I was standing on a trash dump in Honduras last week and I thought of you."

I replied with a sarcastic, "Wow. Thanks buddy!"

He said, "No, that sounded weird. I didn't mean for you to take that the wrong way. I didn't know if you were looking for a location for your college students to take a mission trip? God laid you on my heart as we were there on an information gathering trip?"

There was really no way for him to have known that, but, in general, he probably figured that we would want to do a mission trip some time in the future.

"But, if you are interested, you should come down and check this place out. Just take a vision trip to see if it would be a fit for your ministry," he continued.

I thanked him, and said that I would pray about it, talk to Jaelle, and get back to him within the month.

We found a video about a ministry that had built a school for the kids living in and around the dump in Tegucigalpa, Honduras. It was the first time we had seen or even really knew of communities that are formed around landfills. It was intriguing, compelling and disturbing all at the same time—the videos and pictures were difficult to view. But I couldn't find anything online that gave me much information about it. It was hard to determine what was going on in the community, what the specific needs were, and if there were opportunities to work with any ministries there.

Since moving to Lakeland, I had become friends with a guy by the name of Michael Barrett. He owned Barrett Creative, a production company in Lakeland. He did some of the most incredible video production I had ever seen from a one-man outfit. Our church had hired and fired him a couple of times to do work for them—this would become comedic on multiple levels for several of us in the near future.

Michael was the guy who produced the national television show for Church at the Mall that Jaelle and I had watched for the year leading up to taking the position with the church. Budget cuts eventually eliminated the television ministry, and Michael along with it. We met each other through Pastor Jay because he had an idea to plant a satellite campus that would air his messages through video. Through that process, Michael and I got to know each other.

Over time, I learned that Michael had the same passion that I did for reaching the least—and the same heart for seeing change within the church. We had looked at the Church at large in the United States and asked if we were really doing what we were supposed to be doing. Looking at all the money churches were spending on expenses we considered not directly related to the biblical mission of the Church, the whole approach seemed off. We both felt that we were entirely too focused on church programs for Christians, and not focused enough on reaching the least, the lost, and the forgotten.

So after learning about the opportunity to go to Honduras, I gave Michael a call. I knew he wanted to use his gift for telling a story through video to further the Kingdom of God. I explained that we were going down to Tegucigalpa, and that I believed there was a pretty big story there to report, and would he like to come. He took some time to pray about it, but a few weeks later he called me and said he was on board. It turned out that this was more of a God thing than we could have possibly imagined. It led to our very first experience with a trash dump community.

Throughout the summer, I continued to feel the call to serve the poor. I began processing the fact that I was really going to Honduras and all of the implications of the trip. John Russell, our church's missions pastor at the time, had taken me on my first international missions trip the year before and was helping me examine the call I was feeling. He was the first to predict that I was going to leave my position with the church to follow a call to global missions.

Somehow, I felt that the Honduras trip was going to be something more than a simple short-term mission trip. One night, around 11:00, I decided to take a walk. I ended up walking around the same block about 25 times while praying and asking God if this was going to be a learning time for me and if something was about to change in our lives. Finally, on my last lap around the neighborhood, the words "Trash Mountain" flashed in my mind very clearly. I had never seen the mountains of garbage or had even thought about forming a ministry until those words flashed in my mind. I went back to the house and told Jaelle what had happened. After hearing everything I said, she made the final decision to go on the trip with me, even though that meant leaving our two-year-old and newborn with their grandparents—a very difficult thing for a young mother to do.

EARS TO HEAR

On the Sunday before the trip to Honduras, I was asked to speak in all three worship services at church. It was an honor to be given the opportunity to share about our upcoming trip with the congregation and to have the church praying for us as we traveled. Before the 11:00 AM service, something in the atmosphere felt different to me. I couldn't pinpoint what the feeling was but thought it might be nerves, since that was the most highly attended Sunday service with around 1,200 people coming to worship.

After the service, I was talking with Pastor Jerry Goodell when I noticed a woman standing with a para-dog waving me over. The woman was deaf, but could speak clear enough for me to understand what she was saying. She told me she was 100%

deaf, but when I had spoken about the kids working, living, and dying in trash that morning, she heard everything I said! Then she handed me a check designated for our Honduras trip. Stunned, I waved Jerry over and had her repeat what she had said. She repeated her original comments and added: "If you continue to serve children who are in need, God will bless everything you do."

Afterwards, I talked with Jerry on the phone, and we both asked the same question: *What was that?* Talk about an interesting version of speaking in tongues. Curious, we checked up on the woman and discovered that she was an occasional member of the deaf ministry at the church and confirmed that she was in fact deaf. We tried to make contact with her from the limited information we had, but we couldn't find her. The church had no address on file. The bank couldn't give us her name for security reasons, and her check had no address on it, just a P.O. Box from Apopka, Florida, about a one-hour drive from Lakeland. And, to my knowledge, she never returned to the church while I was on staff. If you are reading this book, please contact me!

This unusual situation put us in the position to expect the unexpected from God. Reflecting back, it is easy to see that the whole Trash Mountain idea could never have been put together simply by a team of creative people. He had moved my family to Florida, given me a passion to serve the poor, put Latin America in my heart, inspired another leader to invite me to Honduras, had put Michael Barrett and me in each other's lives, gave my wife the vision to come with me, and now He had made a deaf daughter of His to hear. The hand of God was undeniably matching up the pieces of the puzzle according to His perfect timing and order, and this was just the beginning.

Chapter 4:

TRASH MOUNTAIN PROJECT

"When the Son of Man comes in his glory, and all the angels with him, then he will sit on his glorious throne. Before him will be gathered all the nations, and he will separate people one from another as a shepherd separates the sheep from the goats. And he will place the sheep on his right, but the goats on the left. Then the King will say to those on his right, 'Come, you who are blessed by my Father, inherit the kingdom prepared for you from the foundation of the world. For I was hungry and you gave me food, I was thirsty and you gave me drink, I was a stranger and you welcomed me, I was naked and you clothed me, I was sick and you visited me, I was in prison and you came to me.' Then the righteous will answer him, saying, 'Lord, when did we see you hungry and feed you, or thirsty and give you drink? And when did we see you a stranger and welcome you, or naked and clothe you? And when did we see you sick or in prison and visit you?' And the King will answer them, 'Truly, I say to you, as you did it to one of the least of these my brothers, you did it to me.'" (Matthew 25:31-40)

A mor Fe y Esperanza (AFE), meaning faith, hope, and love, was founded and led by Pastor Jeony Ordoñiez and his family in 2001. Their mission is to bring faith, hope, and love to the children of the Tegucigalpa, Honduras garbage dump. They are a Honduran-led development project enabling the families of the Tegucigalpa garbage dump to experience the abundant life described by Jesus. They do this by providing the children with education, nutrition, and discipleship training among other things.

Five people went on the trip to visit Amor Fe y Esperanza: Michael Barrett, Ron Gunter, Jerry Haag, Jaelle, and I. Although we were unsure of the direction that the trip was going to take, it became clear to us when we arrived at AFE.

Arriving on a Saturday, we attended Pastor Jeony's church on Sunday; on Monday and Tuesday, we visited AFE so that we could observe the kids throughout a typical day in a trash dump community. We followed them through their school day, documenting everything we could. We were blown away by how the children worshiped the Lord both at the school and at their church. Their faith was so simple yet so powerful.

As we were standing in the community, a little boy ran up to Jeony and said, "Pastor...guess what God did for us yesterday! He provided my father enough items to sell from the dump that we got to eat rice and beans last night!"

The three of us just looked at each other and literally had nothing to say. We were floored by what this child had just said. It really put into perspective some of the trivial things we worry and even pray about, but this kid...rice and beans. Wow!

THE WELL

The dump is located across a highway from AFE. Behind the school runs a creek full of hepatitis and other dangerous bacteria and diseases. People use it for bathing, washing clothes—and sometimes even to drink before AFE put in a fresh-water well. Because of the runoff from the dump, it is no surprise that there is a lot of contamination in the water in the surrounding area.

AFE had a supporter who paid to dig a well for them because there was no fresh-water supply at the school or in the surrounding community. The crew began drilling and hit an aquifer at a much shallower depth than they expected. It looked as though they were going to have their well sooner than they thought! However, they were concerned that because the well was shallow and was so close to the trash dump, it would be contaminated by the runoff.

Before they could use the well, they needed to have someone from the city come out to test the water and approve it. There was a possibility that it would be so contaminated that it could only be used for showering—if even that. When the city worker tested the purity of the water, he reported to Jeony that the water in the well was 100% pure! He said that he had never seen clean water anywhere that close to the landfill. He went on to say that he had felt bad coming out to test their water to begin with because he was sure it was not going to be usable. Now the entire community drinks from that well! Upon asking Jeony about it, he just smiled. It was definitely a miracle. They prayed for clean water and God gave it to them.

LIVE THE COMMAND

Before going to Honduras we had some idea of what we would encounter when we arrived at AFE, but we were not prepared for the journey God had taken us on. When we first set foot on the dump, it was like seeing Matthew 25 come to life: the naked, the sick, the hungry, the thirsty, the lonely, and the criminal all in one physical location.

This famous statement from Jesus at the end of His ministry had haunted me for years. Even though I was a pastor, or what I jokingly referred to as a "professional Christian," I wasn't really doing much of anything on this list. I fully understood that this was not necessarily a comprehensive list of what it looked like to follow Jesus, but it was sure something He felt was important enough to mention at such a crucial juncture of His ministry and teaching.

In addition, was I seeing an opportunity to support and serve Christ's disciples, such as Jeony? To partner with God's chosen leaders within such high-need communities was a great opportunity.

GOOD WORD: TO SERVE
~ DR. JIM CONGDON

Matthew 25:31-46 is surely the most famous passage in the Bible on caring for the needy. Even the mainstream media regularly cite Jesus' command to welcome the stranger, feed the hungry, and clothe the naked. Calls for "social justice" and increased government spending on the needy take for granted that this is what Jesus meant by "the least of these." Those who care for the needy go to heaven, those who don't care go to hell. That's what Jesus is saying, right?

While this is the popular view, Bible students and commentators throughout history have recognized that "the least of these my brothers" refers not to the needy in general, but to the needy of the disciples in particular. The evidence for this is overwhelming: When Jesus speaks of his brothers, he's never referring to the people of the world, but always referring to his followers (see Matthew 12:46-50; 23:8-9; 28:10). And the parallel passage in Matthew 10:40-42 (NIV) clinches it: "He who receives you receives me, and he who receives me receives the one who sent me. Anyone who receives a prophet because he is a prophet will receive a prophet's reward...And if anyone gives even a cup of cold water to one of these little ones because he is my disciple, I tell you the truth, he will certainly not lose his reward."

51

So as you can see, this is pretty much the opposite of the popular view. Jesus is not telling us that we can see his image in the faces of the poor, but that we can see his image in the faces of his family members. Nor is he dangling eternal punishment in front of his disciples if they don't care for the poor, but in front of the world if they don't receive his disciples with their message of salvation. Let's remind ourselves that Jesus came to earth to fix man's relationship to God, not his economic condition. His mission was to save his people from their sins (1:21), not from their hunger.

Does this mean that unbelievers should not receive our mercy? Not at all. In fact, Jesus is adamant elsewhere that we should also help anyone who is in need. For if we love only those who love us, and show mercy only to our brothers and sisters, we are acting no differently than the rest of the world (Luke 6:27-36). "Love your neighbor as yourself," Jesus said. Someone asked, "Who is my neighbor?" Jesus replied by telling the story of the Good Samaritan (Luke 10:2-37). "Your neighbor," Jesus explained in the parable, "is anyone whose need you see, whose need you are able to meet." The apostle Paul puts it all together when he says, "Do good to all people, especially to those who belong to the family of believers" (Galatians 6:10, NIV).

Trash Mountain Project does "all of the above." It obeys Jesus' words to assist both Jesus' disciples and unbelievers alike. It goes to trash dump communities around the world, finds Christian leaders—Jesus' emissaries, in Matthew 25 terms— and empowers them by building churches and schools and businesses to bring lost, hungry children and families out of the dump. TMP exists to see the children and families of the dump rescued, fed, educated, employed, and bound for heaven.

It was hard to come to grips with what we were seeing. There were babies left in boxes and three-year-olds sitting unattended, not sure what to do while watching parents and siblings work in the trash dump—sorting recyclables and anything they could sell for a meager wage. We saw sad faces with empty eyes on all of the kids. I had never seen total emptiness inside such young children. They had been stripped of all innocence.

While shooting the documentary, Michael got hit on the head with an orange someone threw at us. Clearly, we weren't wanted at the dump, especially with our cameras, and we felt very unsafe. We were told that many criminals fled to the dump to work while evading the authorities, so it became a safe haven for some of the most dangerous people in that society. This fact, along with the organized crime, gang activity, and drug use at the dump made us a perfect target for robbery or even worse. We had been warned by Jeony to stay together and keep our eyes open and be aware of our surroundings.

Another time, we were nearly crushed by a truck sliding sideways as the trash below its wheels gave way. This happened right after being told how common it is for children to be crushed and killed under the giant tires of the dump trucks coming and going—and not being found until hours later. If you don't get out of the way, don't expect the trucks to move out of your way.

Flying over the mountain of trash were hundreds of vultures, circling the area, looking for a scrap of food or flesh to eat, and creating an eerie atmosphere. Added to that was the billowing smoke, slave-like people dragging themselves through their day, a horrible sulfur-like smell, and the worst evils the human mind can imagine—it was the very image of what we imagine hell would be like.

But, what impacted us the most was the feeling of hopelessness that pervaded the dump community. Watching three- and four-year-olds rummaging through the trash, collecting scraps and bits to recycle to make a few pesos so they could eat their next meal was something that never leaves you.

ARE YOU PAYING ATTENTION?

In one of the homes we visited lived a family of six: mother, father, grandma, a baby, and two young children. The family had just lost a baby to malnutrition shortly before we arrived. They had an 18-month-old child who was so emaciated and malnourished that he couldn't even lift his head. The mother was feeding him something that we didn't recognize. We found out later that it was curdled Tang that had literally started fermenting. The baby also was fed coffee grounds and water or whatever else the family could find in the hope that he could absorb some nutrition.

The house was about 8 x 8 feet square, and the dirt floor was covered with feces from puppies along with other garbage. The father was not able to leave his family to work the dump because he needed to stay and protect them from some people who had threatened their lives. Because of this, the family was not getting fed. I recall thinking *I've never been in such a difficult and disgusting situation! What can even be done? This is absolutely overwhelming and heart-breaking.*

The father had heard that I was a pastor. He approached me with tears in his eyes and said, "I have faith in Jesus Christ and believe that He can help my family. I know you are a pastor. Will you pray for my family?"

I knelt to pray, surrounded by that beautiful family, but during the prayer I had to stop, overwhelmed by the situation. I didn't know what to say. I was coming from an existence of comfort—never facing such severe hardship. Yet there we were praying for them because they knew I was a pastor and because they knew Jesus could change their lives. I tried to finish the prayer but broke down crying. I hugged each one in the house and apologized for not holding it together. They were all crying too.

I said later that this was the most Holy Spirit-filled prayer of my life, yet I'm not even sure what I said. For me, it was a turning point in my relationship with Christ—when I realized that there was more that I could do besides simply praying over a desperate family. It was as if Jesus was sitting in the room, staring at me and asking, "What are you going to do? Are you going to simply pray and walk away?"

In the midst of what I saw as complete desperation, the family knew that God could change their destiny. That kind of faith seemed incredible in the face of such circumstances. That encounter was as if God flat out hit me in the face and said, "Do this. And don't you dare walk away." We were all disturbed by what we had seen. It was very much an "Are you paying attention?" moment.

INJUSTICE

We went back to AFE and sat in front of the school in silence. The three of us didn't know what to do or say. Shortly after that we sat down with Jeony and asked him to tell us about the situation facing the children and families in the dump, because it was hard for us to comprehend that conditions like that even existed in the world. We asked what things burdened him that he had seen. With tears in his eyes, he told us story—after story—about black market abortions that were being done at the dump, and about the young kids finding body parts from these abortions and whole dead bodies also. Women who endured the abortions would die of infection because of how and where it was done. Kids were raped, and young girls 11- and 12-years-old prostituted themselves to the truck drivers and others who came to the dump.

We talked to a girl who told us that prostitution was the only way she could make money and that her dad wanted her to do it. As a dad, I didn't know how to respond. She would get fifty cents a trick. She was selling her body for fifty cents! And if she didn't, her dad would do similar acts to her himself and beat her for not bringing home that fifty cents.

To see such a young child absolutely demoralized by the situation and the decisions the family was forced to make was beyond difficult. Yet you saw girls everywhere facing the same dilemma. Jeony told us about girls he knew who were being raped on a daily and nightly basis at home or out in the dump. There was no control whatsoever on what these kids had to face.

We met one such father after spending some time with his 11-year-old daughter. He was very drunk, and I was very angry. Standing with him near a cliff presented me with an interesting dilemma. I looked at my wife, and she was shaking her head saying "no" with her eyes. She knew what I was thinking of doing. I don't have to say that that would have been wrong, but it would have been so right on other levels. I am not proud of my thoughts, but it is what it is. I am just trying to be honest about the anger that was burning inside of me, and I believe many fathers would feel the same rage that I did in that moment.

Boys were being beaten, introduced to drugs, and joining gangs just to survive. We talked to young men 16- or 17-years-old who had gone through that, but then saw AFE as a way out. It offered them a safe haven. They were able to go to AFE and break the cycle that had controlled their family for generations. It was rough yet encouraging to see how change can happen.

We talked to a mom who sold her 10-year-old daughter for a cell phone—one that she couldn't even afford to activate. She thought her daughter would still be around, but she was gone. And the mom had no idea where her child was. There was story after story of other kids disappearing to kidnapping and trafficking. There were stories of gang rape where multiple men would abuse a child for an entire evening. They called it a "party."

It is one thing to see starvation and malnutrition, lack of clean water, and other health concerns. It is totally different to see pure evil staring you in the face. That is what we saw in the communities we were beginning to investigate. I can't share all of the gory stories, but it was almost like we were experiencing PTSD (post-traumatic stress disorder) from what we had seen and heard. There was no way to even process the information—we didn't want to share with others and ruin them, and talking about some of the stuff we saw only made it worse at least in my own mind.

Having children of our own made that whole experience hit close to home for Jaelle and I. What made those children any different than ours? Nothing makes them any different. It is just that we seem to pour our resources into a privileged few and let the rest fall by the wayside. We were seeing kids as young as our own raised with the understanding that they are a part of the dump—untouchable to the point that they are no more than part of the garbage around them.

We didn't know if we could make a difference in their world, but we deeply needed God to show us a way to do just that. We knew that over time we would see all those things again, but we also knew that God had given us a light to share in those communities.

DON'T MOVE DOWN HERE

Our last evening in Honduras, Jaelle and I agreed that we were supposed to do more than what we had initially accomplished on the trip. We knew the short documentary that we had created with Michael would be a huge support in bringing awareness to the problem and to AFE. And we knew that AFE would be a great place to bring our young adult ministry, but the call obviously was stronger for us.

When we brought the matter to Pastor Jeony—offering our family to his ministry, and asking how we could best serve at AFE, he said, "The way is not to move down here." He warned us not to take that the wrong way, because he meant it as an encouragement, and he continued, "This is what I mean by this, from what I am told, you are a pastor at a large church in America. You have resources and influence that we can't even imagine. If you can use the influence you have, please do so. Because if people like you don't tell the church about this injustice, and if you don't help," he said, pointing at a young man, "that guy dies Thursday."

His message was heard loud and clear. Here I was, a big white boy who grew up in Middle America suburbia and didn't know a lick of Spanish ... what impact could I possibly have if I moved my family there? But, I do know people in the United States—people with and without faith in Christ who would care about this injustice. This is a human thing. It is a disgrace that this kind of thing happens in our world, and it must stop!

With his words, Jeony had unknowingly launched a global ministry that would eventually reach multiple countries and many similar trash dump communities. He had also given Trash Mountain Project one of its core values: that we are not a sending organization in the traditional sense. Meaning that we don't necessarily plant missionaries in foreign lands—we act more as a silent partner behind the scenes connecting God's Church and His people from the United States to the people and communities we serve. There is inevitably someone like Jeony in each community God has sent us to, someone praying that God would send help, and we humbly pray that He would see fit to use us to answer such a prayer in any way He sees fit.

LORD, SEND ME!

Prayer had become a big part of our young adult ministry, and for me personally, a much bigger part of my life and journey with Christ. I remember reading the book, *Praying* by J.I. Packer and being inspired to learn all that I could from other prayer warriors past and present. When I took the young adult pastor position and was given the keys to the old movie theater to renovate, I made the request to have a prayer room. I wanted a secluded space that was dedicated to prayer. I had fallen in love with the prayer room at Asbury, and I wanted to take elements of that place and others I had seen and build one for our students and church.

After finishing that special room, I found that I really enjoyed and coveted my time spent within its walls. A short time after returning from Honduras, I went into the prayer room and knelt down next to the globe that was on a small table at the back of the space. I began praying. At one point I opened my eyes to see that Honduras was facing me on the globe. I broke down in tears. This was one of the first times I had allowed myself to really process what we had experienced during our time in Honduras.

I embraced a racing thought I had been having in which I tried to imagine what God sees. Have you ever done that? Can you imagine? It overwhelmed me to an extent that I felt that I was going to actually black out. I felt a literal pain in my chest.

Was this a small glimpse at how we should shoulder the weight of the cross? Was I finally getting it? Through my tears, I prayed a prayer that I believe changed the entire path of my life. I have said many times that Trash Mountain Project started with a prayer, and this is the very prayer that I spoke to my Heavenly Father:

"Father, please give me the opportunity to serve You through serving Your people living in trash dump communities all over the world. I will dedicate myself and my family to this work. Please show me what You have for me, and open the doors for Trash Mountain Project to move forward to share Your love and Gospel throughout the world. Please do something so big that we will all see Your glory in ways that we will hardly believe, and that will build our faith stronger every day. I want to witness Your Son's glory in the darkest corners of Your creation. I will die for You, I will die for my family, I will die for my friends, and I will die for whatever You ask of me. Give me the courage to follow You no matter what—not only in this ministry, but with my family, friends, and enemies alike. My life is Yours Lord, send me."

That was it. Not long. Not eloquently spoken. But it was from my soul, and I meant every word of it. After praying that prayer, I felt a tremendous sense of peace pour over me. God's Spirit filled that room and comforted me in a way that assured me that He was with me and would illuminate my path as long as I was dedicated to His work. It was a transformational moment in my life.

Jesus had been dedicated to all of us since long before we were here, and it was time I did my best to follow His divine lead. The words spoken in Matthew 25 and all throughout His Word were not for my entertainment or simply for my study. They are meant to instruct and lead our action in faith.

Upon leaving the prayer room, I went to the office of my close friend and ministry partner, Bill Horn, and poured my heart out about what was happening in my life. I will always remember his encouragement and support from the very beginning of this ministry, even when it sounded impossible and even illogical. He said, "Brett, there is no doubt in my mind what is going on. There is no doubt that this is what God wants from you. Follow Him, and know that I will always have your back."

GOOD WORD: WHAT DOES GOD SEE? ~ DR. JIM CONGDON

The Bible tells us that "...the Lord sees not as man sees..." (1 Samuel 16:7). That's a fact. But, as Brett's life story illustrates, God takes steps to bring us to the place where we see what He sees. For when we see what He sees, we suddenly care about what He cares about.

Jonah is a great illustration of this. Though he was a prophet of God, he cared only for himself and "his kind of people." He couldn't care less about lost people far away in the city of Nineveh. After all, they were Israel's enemies! Jonah couldn't have been happier when God told him to go to Nineveh and preach, "Forty more days and Nineveh will be overthrown" (Jonah 4:4, NIV).

Jonah never stopped to wonder—if God simply wants to destroy those foreigners, why the 40 days? The answer was that when God looked at Nineveh, He saw something Jonah didn't see. God saw lost people, and lost people matter to God. And God felt compassion, and gave them 40 days to hear the message and respond.

They did respond, with overwhelming repentance. God was happy, and decided to spare them. You would think that Jonah would be happy too, but he wasn't. Jonah didn't have God's eyes, and so he didn't have God's heart.

Ask yourself: Do I see what God sees? Do I have a heart for what moves God's heart? God's goal for us, as for Jonah, is to get us to see what He sees, so that we will care about what He cares about.

THE BASEBALL CONFIRMATION

Several days later, we went to Jaelle's mom's house for Thanksgiving. We were spiritually, emotionally, and physically wrecked from the trip and acknowledged that we knew we ought to be doing something more, we just didn't know what. We began praying and discussing the possibility of Trash Mountain becoming a full-fledged stand-alone ministry. While we were talking about this, we agreed that we needed some sort of confirmation, and to seek wise counsel before making any major decisions.

As I said those words to Jaelle, my phone chimed from a new text. I didn't take the time to look at it as Jaelle and I were in a pretty deep conversation. And, after a couple of hours of discussion, we decided to go to bed. Restless and unable to sleep, I decided to go for a walk, forgetting about the unread text on my phone. I prayed during the walk for confirmation to launch Trash Mountain Project. When I returned, I remembered the text I had forgotten to check. It was a message from Paul Byrd, who was on a camping trip in Georgia with his family.

Paul was a professional baseball player with the Cleveland Indians who had been a guest speaker with our young adult ministry the previous spring. He was near Lakeland for spring training when he agreed to speak to our students. On Wednesday, August 6, 2008, I arranged to meet with him after a game he played against the Tampa Bay Rays. Well, actually I had hit him up for free tickets to the game as he had offered to hook me up when they played Tampa. After the game, he took Jaelle and I out to dinner in St. Petersburg, and, in a matter of minutes, we ended up talking about the Trash Mountain "idea." Paul became interested right away and wanted to jump on board with us.

When I received the text message from him that Thanksgiving night, we had not talked since that dinner back in August. He had been thinking about me, Jaelle, and TMP and wondered how he could get involved. Feeling an urge to contact me, he sent a text inquiring about Trash Mountain at the exact moment I had prayed for confirmation. He was in the woods in Georgia praying and was led to text me with his family's support. The incredible timing of someone contacting me about a ministry that didn't even exist yet, at the exact timing of Jaelle and I discussing confirmation, had to belong to God. By now, I had begun to abandon the concept of coincidences in my life.

WHAT COULD A VIDEO REALLY DO?

After our trip to Honduras, Jonathan Olive, a professional film editor, and yet another previous staff member at Church at the Mall, teamed up with Michael to put the nine-minute Honduras documentary together. The short documentary was simply named *Trash Mountain Project*. It was sent to AFE and several of their partner ministries for use in telling the story and raising awareness and resources to enact change at the trash mountain Honduras site.

I had always had a deep interest in storytelling, whether it was through books, movies, or the spoken word. But, the public response to the video that Michael and Jonathan put together was overwhelming—people really wanted to help.

Michael had always been confident that storytelling via video could change the world, and I was beginning to believe him. Pastor Chris Gooding, and the children's ministry at our church even decided to raise money to try and build a house for one of the families at AFE after seeing the video. In just seven weeks, the kids were able to raise $7,200—enough to build two homes and house five adults and 11 children! As a result of their faithfulness and answering a need in the way that they did, Leili's story of redemption took place just seven months later.

LEILI

We met Leili when we were in Honduras for our first trip in the fall of 2008. Many times on mission trips there are several kids around the ministry who will follow us around or that we will get to know better than some of the others. Ten-year-old Leili was one of those who tagged alongside Jaelle and Michael and me on our first trip to Tegucigalpa. We enjoyed having her with us and getting to know about her and her family. Through her lack of words and body language, you could tell she had been through a lot and had seen even more in her short life.

We asked Pastor Jeony how we could help as a US-based ministry partnering with international ministries doing the on-the-ground work with locals in each community. It was apparent in Honduras that a great need was to assist with home building. Our first trip after officially forming TMP was in December 2009 with a team that had the task of building two homes. About a month before the trip we heard that one of the homes we would be building was for Leili's family. There had been some adverse circumstances that required them to get into a new living situation sooner than later.

When we arrived, Pastor Jeony pulled me aside and said, "I need to talk to you about Leili. She has been having a really hard time. We know you got to know her on your first trip here and we wanted to let you know that a couple of months ago we found that she was at her wits end and ready to give up on life. We convinced her not to give up, and she came to see a counselor to try and get the help she so obviously needed. What would drive Leili to this? She shared that she was afraid to sleep in her own home because there was no protection from the outside. And then we realized there were probably some significant issues going on at home. The structure of Leili's current home—without any doors with locks—didn't provide any security. It couldn't even really be called a home, it was just a lean-to shack. Rain constantly runs through the area where she sleeps, and she is simply exhausted."

Pastor Jeony said that in the process of working with Leili and explaining that she was going to get a new home, he had asked her if she remembered those people with the cameras, Michael, Brett, and Jaelle. She said that she did. But it was what she said next that changed us forever. When Pastor Jeony explained that we were coming back down to build her a new home and asked what she thought of that, her response was, "You mean God really does hear my prayers?"

Wow! God had answered Leili's prayer and permanently convinced her that He was there and that He does-in-fact hear her prayers. Additionally, this was the first extreme example of God using TMP to be an answer to someone else's prayer. Over the years, we have gotten to know Leili better. She is 15 years old and is an incredible young lady who has become one of the top students at AFE. Things have changed for her. Providing a small place to live for her family had such an impact. This story encouraged us on multiple levels, not the least of which was that we were on the right path. There is never going to be a perfect way to do things as a ministry, but, in this instance, there was a little girl who saw a clear answer to prayer, and it taught her that God really did hear her when she prayed.

Chapter 5:

WHAT NOW?

———— •◦• ————

We knew we could help by sending teams to build houses and complete other projects in partnership with AFE, but we were also aware that what we saw in Honduras was probably a global problem. So I started doing research on trash dump communities, and began calling people I respected for wise counsel concerning Trash Mountain Project.

At no point did I ever feel like I was supposed to start a new organization or mission. It was more of a "how do we go about a partnership?" thought. I was still a pastor at a church, and I had a ministry I was already dedicated to leading...and yet everything in me started shifting. There was really no way to fight the reality that my passion was evolving from young adult ministry to serving the poor and the development of trash dump communities.

As I researched through simple internet searches, I found trash dump communities all over the world. We had already begun planning a trip to the Phnom Penh, Cambodia, landfill, and it dawned on me that this might be turning into more than just a side project or part of our young adult ministry. We needed to examine who was out there, and what was going on with any similar ministries.

As I was seeking to find someone who specialized in trash dump communities, and who was based here in the United States so that we could speak, I literally couldn't find a single ministry with such communities as their entire focus. I found organizations and churches that were doing work within trash dump communities as a part of what they do, but there was no one solely focused on it. To me, it seemed like such a unique segment of society, an entire sub-culture within developing and underdeveloped countries, and I found it odd that there was no one for whom this was their focus.

SEEKING WISE COUNSEL

In March 2009, I had a conversation with Dr. Russell West, who had been my professor at Asbury Theological Seminary. I have a deep respect for him, and my questions fell right into his area of expertise, cross-cultural and organizational leadership. We had loosely kept in touch after I finished seminary and moved to Florida, so I called him and asked his thoughts about all that we were experiencing in our lives. His advice was that we shouldn't start anything new unless we absolutely had to. One reason to do so would be if there was no one else to join who was already doing that kind of mission really well.

Dr. West's advice was solid, and I took it to heart and prayed about it. I kept looking, trying to find someone who was doing this in order to join them, but knowing that if I didn't find anyone, I needed to think it through and continue to pray before launching a new organization.

Dr. West warned me how hard it was to start a new organization—a lot like a church plant, which has to be one of the most difficult endeavors that exist. It would have been made even more difficult at that time because the U.S. economy was hitting the skids, and we were in one of the hardest-hit states: Florida. It obviously takes financial support to begin an organization that will have a global impact, so how was this going to work if we moved forward?

I talked to my parents, who had always supported me in following God's call on my life. I discussed it with my brother, Derek, whom I have a great relationship with and a deep respect for. They basically said the same thing as Dr. West and told me to be in prayer about it and that if I felt God releasing me and telling me to do it, then go for it.

I talked with Joe Hishmeh, lead pastor of Fellowship Bible Church in Topeka, and he said the same thing. Yet there was also the advice I was getting from a lot of other people who meant well, but thought it was a bad idea. They definitely had my family's best intentions at heart, but said things like: "That is probably not the best choice. You know what I mean? Do you really want to start a new nonprofit organization? Do you know what that process is like? What if something happened to you? What about your family?"

Over the following month, even though there was a lot of doubt expressed that we should do this, Jaelle, Michael and I decided to at least take the step to incorporate. I felt that most of the doubt was grounded in worldly concerns, not Christ-centered mission. I truly believed that this was God's call, not mine. I was just a tool that He was planning to use to begin this work.

So, we formed a Board of Directors: Michael Barrett, Joshua Bechard (who later became TMP's full-time IT Director), Jaelle, and I. On April 6, 2009, we moved ahead and incorporated in the state of Florida. God brought an incredible CPA into our lives, Ben Fairchild, who helped us prepare our 501(c)3 application and eventually became our independent CPA. In late May 2009, we submitted our Form 1023 to the IRS, expecting to wait up to a year for a response.

Jaelle soon coined the motto: "Live the Command" for TMP. We were called to live Christ's command to go out into the entire world to share the Gospel and love others in the way He taught us through His life and ministry.

As Jaelle and I had prayed about the ministry in the months prior, and now had officially launched it, we promised each other that we would leave Church at the Mall by January 2010. Little did we know that that our relationship with this church would end just a few short weeks later.

PUSHED OUT OF THE NEST

It was during the time of development about a year before the Honduras trip that I had heard of Legacy of Hope International (LOHI) through a couple of friends who attended our young adult worship service and had become involved with the ministry in Lakeland. LOHI served the poor in Cambodia and knew of another trash dump community there that was in desperate need.

In early 2009, I met with Tim Brown, president of LOHI. He told us that Phnom Penh, Cambodia, had one of the largest trash dump communities in the world, situated right in the heart of the city for over 40 years. Generations of people had lived, worked, and died in that dump. The landfill was so unstable that kids would fall through holes where the trash had been burning from the bottom up. Their feet would touch the embers and their flesh would burn. I asked Tim if we could shoot a documentary about the dump community on his next trip to Cambodia. We believed that this could help the ministries working there to raise awareness and resources, just as we had already seen in such a short time in Honduras.

I presented a possible trip to Cambodia and the call I felt from God on my life to my direct boss, the missions pastor, and then, over lunch, with Pastor Jay. I didn't say that I wanted to do it full time yet. I felt God's calling to serve children and families living in trash dump communities, but was still praying if this was the best move for my family. Jay was 100% supportive, and even told me that anything or anyone who tried to stop me was from Satan. He said that I had to travel to Cambodia to learn more about the problem and see what could be done. All three pastors gave me their blessing to take personal time off for the trip.

Everything went smoothly, except that I didn't talk directly with our new executive pastor. I figured that since I had permission from his boss, the senior pastor, there would not be a problem. But he was actually angry that I had talked with Jay directly instead of going through him. He soon vetoed the idea making the statement that, "you are not to go directly to Jay about something that I am unaware of, because I was caught off guard when he mentioned it in our meeting today. Additionally, you were hired to bring college students and young adults into this church, not to travel around the world visiting kids living in trash."

And during the meeting where he said this, I looked over at my direct boss, Mark, who was the only other person in the room hearing those ridiculous words coming out of the mouth of a pastor. Mark looked frustrated, his eyes focused on the ground. I think he knew what was coming, and wanted to protect me as his friend and ministry partner, but was stuck in a really bad spot, because part of the statement we had just heard was true—I was the young adult pastor, not the missions pastor.

That was the beginning of the end of my position at the church. There was no way I could serve under the leadership of someone who would make such statements, and, on a personal note, I don't think he liked me much, either. There are many ways to "do" ministry in the Christian Church, and we definitely had our differences. I had gotten along so well with our previous executive pastor, and this just wasn't working out. Our feelings for each other had just become mutual.

Several weeks later, I was called into the executive pastor's office and fired from my position. The entire executive staff was there except for Jay and Dave McClamma, the missions pastor at the time. The executive pastor was basically the only one who spoke, and the first thing out of his mouth was that the young adult ministry was going to continue moving on, but that I would no longer be a part of it. It was a pretty brutal way to tell me that I was fired. His explanation was that the church was restructuring and they had no more need for a young adult pastor.

They allowed me to quietly resign, and offered to pay my salary through August, which was very helpful as we were trying to figure out how to move forward in what God had planned for our family. For me, it was hard to leave my church and the young adult ministry I had founded and dedicated my life to for the prior two-and-a-half years, but it was all in God's timing and ended up being one of the best things that has ever happened to me.

Because Jay was not in this meeting, they reassured me that he had approved my termination. My mind shot back to my conversation with Jay two months prior where he told me that anything that got in the way of this call was from Satan. I was not really sure what to think of this. But, since that time, Jay has written me a letter apologizing for how my departure from the church was handled. I appreciated him reaching out to me, which brought closure to all that had transpired. Today, I can honestly say that I still love him and the people at Church at the Mall. It was a painful experience, but it was all part of God's master plan.

Although I could have found a job at another church, after a great deal of prayer I decided to continue pursuing TMP at least through the upcoming Cambodia trip, which happened to be the next week. It was during this time I coined what I have referred to as the "fearful peace" settling in on me. [My definition of "fearful peace" is the sense that everything was going to work out and that TMP was the right thing to do at the right time... despite not knowing exactly how it was all going to work out.]

Chapter 6:

A GIRL NAMED CRICKET

M ichael and I, as well as our two friends from Legacy of Hope International (LOHI), traveled to Cambodia from June 14 to 26, 2009. The first six or seven days we toured around the country, visiting some of the tourist sites and seeing a lot of what was going on in the LOHI ministry locations. Michael and I began really questioning why we were there, since we hadn't even seen the trash dump community yet and that was the whole reason for our trip.

One of the days we visited Siem Riep, a popular tourist attractions in Cambodia. There were little kids everywhere, begging for themselves, and for their parents, or working for a pimp. As the team was walking over a huge bridge, I saw a little girl about six years old holding what appeared to be a doll.

Michael and I walked up to the girl, and I turned to him and said, "Dude, that's a baby. That's a real baby!" Michael had thought it was a doll as well, but we could see that it was a tiny newborn girl whose skin was roasted from the hot sun. She looked dead. Her eyes were rolled back, the whites of the eyes had turned yellow, and it was obvious that she was within hours or days of dying. The six-year-old girl was holding the baby to elicit pity from tourists.

Our group gave her a couple of dollars and watched her run away with the baby's head flopping all over the place. She ran to her mother who was nearby on a bicycle and gave her the money. The small family then got on the bicycle and were about to ride away when our team approached them and began to speak with the mother.

After we were done with the interview, someone suggested that we pray for the woman. As we began praying, Michael and I locked eyes. We each knew what the other was thinking: *What is happening here?* The prayer concluded, and we let the mom and her daughters leave. Everyone was really quiet as we got into the van, and in true American tourist fashion, drove to a nice restaurant for dinner. As we sat down at the table and began ordering our food, I got up and walked off to be alone. I found a private area by a river behind the restaurant, sat down, and tears began streaming down my cheeks.

I started questioning God, asking how that little girl could be treated so poorly. Up until then, we had been trying to figure out why we had even come to Cambodia, and, at that moment, it was beginning to seem as though that little girl might be the whole reason. I continued to pray, *God, don't let me walk away from a situation like that ever again in my life! Please let us help that baby and her family. We just don't know what to do or how to do it. Please give us the opportunity.*

After about 20 minutes, I went back into the restaurant. Everyone was absolutely silent, so taken by what had happened. Michael turned to me and said, "What the hell is the point of prayer?" I knew that something serious was going through Michael's head. I had never seen him so upset. It wasn't that we had seen anything worse than before. What was so troubling was the fact that we had simply prayed for this dying child's family and walked away to fatten ourselves up on another big dinner.

At the hotel that night, I was so disturbed that I struggled to fall asleep. The next morning, Michael and I went down to breakfast and talked about what had gone on the previous day. Michael said, "I agreed with God last night that I don't ever again want to pray a prayer that I'm not willing to be the answer to." Not that he necessarily is *going* to be the answer, but that he is not *willing* to be the answer that God chooses.

After talking about it some more, we decided to forgo our previous plans and return to the spot where we had seen the baby and do something to help her. We started asking around and found out that she lived in another village. We drove to the village and asked around again, finally locating the mother who was out working with the baby. We found her and learned that the baby was only a month old. The woman's husband worked, but only made 50 cents to a dollar a day and didn't have much money for food. They lived in a small lean-to shack.

We explained that she could not work with her baby like that because it might ultimately lead to her daughter's death. We took them into our van because there was a crowd gathering around us. We asked how much she earned. She replied that she made around a dollar a day. Our team offered to pay her a dollar or two a day to not work with her baby and instead to stay home and take care of her children. Her face immediately brightened up, and she accepted our help.

The help would continue after we went home. TMP partnered with the local church in her area to be the point of contact with her. We sponsored the little girl through LOHI. Her name in Khmer means Cricket, so that is what we called her.

After setting the family up with the assistance they needed, *then* we prayed with them. We wanted her to understand that we were not just some Americans with money coming to help her, but that it was God who had sent us. We told her about Christ and prayed with her. She understood what we were trying to say and thanked Jesus for everything.

When I had prayed at the restaurant, it was clear that God was saying that we were His people and were supposed to help His children. And then He gave us the opportunity to do just that. Following our trip, we received reports and pictures back that a church had since been planted in that community. Pictures of Cricket came back to us. She's grown and is healthy and doing great. Her family has gotten additional help from us to rebuild their home. They can afford baby formula now and can feed all of their children.

God gave us the opportunity to help, but we walked away. I truly believe that God answered our prayer for that little girl by convicting all of us to take action. We came back and corrected our mistake. In the end, we walked away thinking that if that was the only reason we were supposed to go to Cambodia, it was worth it. Michael's mother, Jackie, commented that "Cricket may be the entire reason you guys are over there." But God had more coming for us than just one precious little girl and her family.

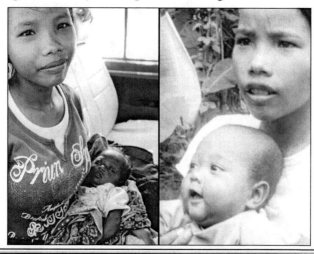

GOOD WORD: BECOME THE ANSWER TO YOUR PRAYERS ~ DR. JIM CONGDON

Sooner or later, every Christian who prays discovers that he or she becomes God's answer to his or her own prayers! This especially happens when we pray for the needy and the lost. Jesus told the Twelve that, "The harvest is plentiful, but the workers are few. Ask the Lord of the harvest, therefore, to send out workers into his harvest field" (Luke 10:2, NIV). And then, without waiting for these "other" workers to show up, Jesus sent the disciples into the harvest field! The Apostle Paul prays (Ephesians 1:15-23) that his readers will come to know God better. And then, he goes on in the next five chapters to help them know God better!

> It's dangerous to pray for the lost, the poor, and the needy. You open your eyes to find that God is going to make you the answer to your own prayer!

AT HOME IN THE DUMP

The last three days of our trip, we finally went to visit the 44-year-old landfill in the capital city of Phnom Penh. When we first walked into the trash dump, we felt at home. It was the strangest thing, because the smell was awful, and it was really the most horrible place we could imagine. It was simply a response to our calling to dump communities.

I can still remember Michael's face as we stood on that mountain of trash. We had no idea what to expect, but we were both happy to be there. I believe this was the first time we joked with each other about being trash pastors. I personally think the funniest thing I have ever been called is "the bishop of trash." It creates a funny mental picture, doesn't it?

The first day, we saw all the same horrors and needs we had discovered in Honduras, just a different locale. The second day was spent filming. We connected with a local pastor who showed us around the community and set us up with individual interviews with some of the families.

Our team got to see some of the homes that the residents lived in and meet some really incredible people. Most of the homes were small one-room shanties built with a combination of scrap wood, billboards, cardboard, and metal. Some families had as many as 12 living in a one-room shack with a leaky roof and runoff from the dump coming through to the mud floor where they all slept.

One mother had six kids: two were in the hospital, two had been taken to an orphanage, and two were working with her in the dump to provide for the family. Interviewing the families, we learned that none of them had any idea what to do to get out of their situation. They knew the dump was going to be moving several miles outside the city at some point, and didn't know what to do as this was the only livelihood they had ever known. More than 1,000 families were displaced when the dump did move to the new site near the famous Choeung Ek killing fields.

Michael's home church provided $1,000 for rice, huge blue plastic tarps to cover the ramshackle homes from the rain, and other amenities. We handed out the supplies on our second day. A government official, the village leader, happened to show up that day. He had never been to the church/school where we were handing out supplies, but came to hand out the rice and tarps to the people to show the people of the dump that the city cared and was trying to help them. It appeared that he was just capitalizing on the opportunity for some positive PR.

Afterword, we spoke with him and asked if there was a plan to aid all of the displaced families upon the moving of the land-fill. There was some backtracking from how proud he was of the work being done in the area, and he had no good suggestion as to where the people would go. But he was pretty proud of cleaning up the eyesore that the dump had become. We sarcastically thought "Wow, well as long as everything is a bit prettier to the eye, all is well."

Night was soon falling. And it would be a night that would change my life and the path of TMP forever.

Chapter 7:

RESCUED FROM DARKNESS

"Rejoice in the Lord always; again I will say, Rejoice. Let your reasonableness be known to everyone. The Lord is at hand; do not be anxious about anything, but in everything by prayer and supplication with thanksgiving let your requests be made known to God. And the peace of God, which surpasses all understanding, will guard your hearts and your minds in Christ Jesus. Finally, brothers, whatever is true, whatever is honorable, whatever is just, whatever is pure, whatever is lovely, whatever is commendable, if there is any excellence, if there is anything worthy of praise, think about these things. What you have learned and received and heard and seen in me— practice these things, and the God of peace will be with you. I rejoiced in the Lord greatly that now at length you have revived your concern for me. You were indeed concerned for me, but you had no opportunity. Not that I am speaking of being in need, for I have learned in whatever situation I am to be content." (Philippians 4:4-11)

W e had been up on the dump for some time, wearing masks because the fumes were so toxic. The trash is always burning, and there is smoke and fumes everywhere that choke you until you can hardly breathe. As darkness was falling, we went back up to the dump to film. From what we had been told, we were the first people to ever film at night. That simple fact should have sent red flags flying for us about the wisdom of our actions, but we are a bit slow, and are many times called "idealists" by our elders.

It's not that we didn't understand that that was a potentially dangerous situation. We had been told by everyone we had talked to from the community that nighttime was when most of the bad things we had been hearing about happened on the dump. So we went along with some teenaged guys from the school where we had handed the rice out to act as our local protection, but even they seemed hesitant.

Traveling up the side of the mountain, we were distracted by a beautiful sunset, and wanted to capture it on film for the documentary. As we filmed, we noticed a massive double rainbow over the dump—even though there were not many clouds and it hadn't rained that day.

After darkness fell, we were taking some final pictures of the sunset before walking over to where the people were scavenging as the trucks dumped their loads. Michael assisted me with the shutter speed on the camera I was using to take a picture of a dump truck that caught our eye as it was coming towards us on the access road we were standing near. It was the last picture we took that evening before the truck curiously pulled up and stopped right in front of us.

The reason this particular truck caught our eye over the hundreds of trucks we had seen was that there was a guy standing on top of the truck, waving and smiling at us. The fact that this man was waving and smiling was odd because most of the time other truck drivers and riders would barely nod, and, at worst, would throw obscene gestures and curse at us. Hey, whoever said there aren't some perks to not knowing the local dialect? They knew that the TMP team was there reporting on the bad condition of their place of work, which wasn't necessarily appreciated.

We were increasingly curious when the truck pulled up to us and stopped. Several men in the cab were saying something to get our attention. Our interpreter, Sam, (originally from the Philippines) began talking with the animated truck driver and others in the cab and then turned around, his face pale. He told us that we had to get out of the dump right away. According to the truck driver, the gang that controlled the dump's criminal element was waiting on the road up ahead to stab us with daggers and take our video equipment.

Immediately, my adrenaline levels reached a record high, and it felt like my blood went cold. Racing thoughts began filling my head. *Were we about to die? What about my family? God, we are here to serve You, where are You?* Looking back, I can understand why they were targeting us. We had camera equipment equal to the annual wages for several people, and who were we to them?

We quickly began making our way down the side of the dump, but immediately noticed two guys following us. I positioned myself in the back of our group. Michael was walking in front of me, and all I heard was him saying, "Jesus, Jesus, Jesus, Jesus..." I was praying a very different prayer, after questioning where God was and begging Him to intervene, I moved on to a compromise, asking Him to give me just one moment as I used to be when I was a troubled teenager with aggressive tendencies. Understand, that when I say aggressive tendencies, I mean that I liked to fight. I had struggled for so many years with my temper, and I knew it was not a character trait that was honoring to God or others around me, but wasn't this a legitimate request?

From my position, I kept an eye on the guy to my left. He was much closer than the other, and he was quickly closing the gap. I could see a large hook in his hand, the kind typically used for sorting through garbage. I also realized that almost every man working at the dump carried a machete.

As we got to the edge of the dump that bordered the community—where the controlling gang resided—I stopped, turned around, and looked back one more time. Honestly, I did this more to get into a defensive position preparing for a fight. The young man to my left had stopped dead in his tracks and was staring at me, frozen, with a strange look on his face. All of a sudden, he turned and nervously walked the other way, looking back over his shoulder.

The other young man following us made a similar move. I couldn't figure out what had made them turn around so suddenly. It wasn't like they had just noticed my size (I am about twice the size of the average Cambodian man), but who cares, they were leaving us alone. I was just thankful we were no longer being followed. We made our way through the village to the tuk tuk (motorized cart) that would take us out of the community. As we drove away unharmed, Michael turned to me and said, "What just happened?" I simply replied, "I think God just saved our lives."

AN UNSEEN VOICE

After returning to the hotel, we wisely decided to not tell our wives what had happened until we were back home. After a long discussion, Michael and I called it a night. I don't believe I can recall a time that I have ever prayed so many prayers of thanksgiving and gratitude to Jesus for His provision and protection, though my prayers quickly turned to questions concerning what I was supposed to do with my life. Was I really supposed to do this full time? How would I care for my own family if I followed this path? And heck, I had just nearly been murdered on my second trip to a trash dump community.

After falling asleep while praying (you know those disrespectful times of passing out while conversing with God), I was startled out of a dead sleep around 3:00 AM by a voice saying, "John 14." Honestly believing that Michael must have said something, I said, "what?" I then realized Michael was sound asleep in the bed next to me. Let's just say the hair was standing up on the back of my neck.

That passage didn't necessarily mean anything to me, and I am not great at memorizing specific passages of Scripture. I'm better with overall concepts throughout the Bible. I felt that I wasn't necessarily crazy, at least not in my opinion. And I knew I wasn't dreaming—the voice startled me as much as if someone had kicked the lights on and yelled "wake up!" I went into the bathroom so that I could get some light, read John 14 and not wake Michael. With tears filling my eyes with every word I read, I decided to write down what God taught me through His Book that night...this is what I wrote:

Tonight, when we were sleeping, I was awoken by God, and He simply told me: "John 14"
Here is what He taught me in this moment...
Jesus had just washed His disciple's feet...
And He goes on to tell us...
Do not be troubled.
Believe in Me.
I go to prepare a place for you.
I am God...no one comes to my Father except through Me.
If you know Me...you know God.
I will do miraculous things through you, if you truly believe in Me.
Whatever you ask of Me to bring glory to My Father, I will do it.
If you love Me, you will do what I command...(Matthew 25 and Honduras flashed in my mind)
I am sending a Helper...and you will never be without Him... Holy Spirit.
He will live inside of you...I will live inside of you.
You will not be orphans...as I am with you always.
I love you.
I will fight for you.
My Spirit will guide you.
I give you peace.
Do not be troubled
Do not be afraid of anything...I am with you.
Evil is coming.
Get up, and do as I have instructed you.

It was more than just an encouraging word. I couldn't imagine reading anything else that would have been more reassuring and more confirming than that He was with us every step of the way. I was convicted about how easily we forget that if we believe in what Jesus promised us, He's with us all the time (see Matthew 28:20). And that should be a very empowering thing. We should never be afraid.

I had been in some really hairy situations throughout my misspent youth, but what I experienced that night at the dump was different. The air felt thick that night, and there was an eerie atmosphere around us. Walking out of the dump alive was really a spiritual experience—even though fear took over, and we felt the opposite at the time, we were not alone! After reading that passage of scripture in the Gospel of John, sitting in the hotel bathroom in Cambodia, I broke down in tears and thanked God for the promise He had made to His people: He would not leave us alone, and He would always fight for His children. He has done so throughout the history of the world, and He is never changing in His promises!

GOOD WORD: ENCOUNTERING GOD ~ DR. JIM CONGDON

This chapter's bathroom encounter with God speaking to Brett out of John 14 is an experience that you can have. In fact, it's one that you should have. How? You simply open the Bible and, prayerfully listening to God speak to you in His word, write down what He is saying to you in your own words. And when you are finished, like Brett, you have in front of you the personal words of God to you. The great saints have called it "reading devotionally," and "making a personal paraphrase of the Bible." You've just come up with your own "Living Bible." Try it.

John 14 played a pivotal role in the formation of Trash Mountain Project, Brett says. And when you read John 14, with Brett's devotional reading next to it (I recommend this), you can see why. It contains at least four of the great themes that have made TMP unique:

(1) We can do greater things for God than we can imagine. 14:12

Jesus says in v. 12, essentially: "Did you know you can do great things for God? You better believe it. In fact, you can do things even greater and more glorious than what I've done, because I'm going to leave earth and return to my Father when I finish my salvation work here. I know that my leaving depresses you right now, but it should excite you, because it means I'll be sending the Holy Spirit Himself down to kick off a brand new era, the final Age. Listen, the Age of the Spirit will be so superior to everything before it, that whatever is done for God in that age is greater than anything that's ever happened before."

(2) Lovers obey, obeyers love. 14:15

Again in my own paraphrase (see, you can do it too!), Jesus is saying: "Your obedience to My commands tells the tale of your love for Me. If you love Me, then you'll obey Me; if you don't obey Me, you don't love Me. Stop singing 'I love You, Lord' until first you say 'I'll obey You, Lord.'"

(3) God discloses Himself to those who truly love Him. 14:21-22

"You want a special 'inside sports' relationship with me and my Father? No problem. We love to open up and disclose Ourselves to those who love Us enough to obey Us. In fact, all three of Us in the Godhead—Father, Son, and Holy Spirit will show Ourselves to those of you who really love Us."

> (4) Don't worry, trust me. 14:1, 27
> "I know your heart is troubled, and no wonder. It's a hostile world out there. Life is hard and then you die. But don't be troubled. Be fearless, because I am with you right now, and I am coming for you one day. You can trust Me. Get up, and do what I tell you."

DON'T YOU DARE DEVIATE

On our last day in Cambodia, we finalized filming and spent the day talking to a couple of the families we had gotten to know within the community, asking them what we could do to help. We experienced no problems and never even saw the gang we encountered at the dump the night before. Thank God. After making the decision to partner with the local leaders at the school we had visited, we gave them some money to assist several of the families with their next month's expenses, with the intention of following up with more permanent assistance in the future. Within a couple of months, we moved one of those families to another location and helped them start a micro-business, with the hope that it would provide a new livelihood outside of the trash dump.

That final night in Cambodia, I found myself filled with anxiety and wrestling with God yet again about whether the Trash Mountain Project thing was what God had in store for the future of my family. I was asking Him to tell me what to do, as I was deeply concerned with how I was going to provide for my family if I continued with the TMP vision. What can I say, I am dense! For the second time in my life, I decided to "put out a fleece" for God's direction. And, for the second straight night, I was startled out of my sleep in the early morning hours.

Sometimes God can speak to you: your heart, your soul, your ears, your eyes—and every sense in your body jumps to attention, and you know it's not human. It is from Him who created you. In this instance, it seemed that every sense was ambushed all at once. He said, "Don't you dare deviate from this path I have you on." And that was it. At that very moment, I committed my family to His call to move forward full-time with TMP. There was no turning back.

After that, the Lord led me to read Philippians 4:4-11. It was the reassurance that God was going to take care of me and provide for my family. Specifically, in verses six–seven, God guides us to not be anxious about anything, remain thankful no matter what, pray, and be at peace resting in the protection of our Father. He was reiterating what He had already promised to me in John 14 the night before. Would I rest in His promises and move forward in faith in His purposes—with confidence? I returned home completely on fire, wanting to continue with the work in Cambodia and with TMP.

After leaving the country on June 25, 2009, Michael and I found ourselves at the Bangkok airport talking about our plans for the documentary. We had originally thought that we were going to shoot a documentary like the one we did in Honduras—finding a ministry and highlighting the work they were doing. But on this trip, we didn't find what we had expected. The story we ended up with was the utter hopelessness of the situation in the Phnom Penh trash dump community. We called the short documentary "Trashed," because the people had no source of hope.

THE PRAYERS OF THE RIGHTEOUS

Upon returning from Cambodia, I reported to work on Sunday morning, June 28 (very jet-lagged and on our sixth wedding anniversary), and bumped into a friend and church co-worker, Brenda Rinier, who wanted to hear about the trip. During our conversation she asked, "What was going on with you and your team on Tuesday morning last week?" I asked her why she asked and Brenda said she had been at her desk and felt God lay us heavily on her heart, that she needed to pray for us right at that moment. She even went on to say that she hadn't prayed for our team in a few days, but that for some reason she just couldn't get us out of her mind that morning, and simply couldn't work until she spent extensive time in prayer.

I didn't make the connection at first, but after figuring in the time difference, I realized that Brenda had been feeling the call to prayer the same night as the dump truck incident. After telling her what had happened, and having the hair on the back of our necks stand at attention, we both felt a sense of awe that God had directed her prayers exactly at our time of desperate need—on the other side of the world!

Throughout that morning at church, two other friends stopped me and asked about Tuesday morning—for similar reasons and using similar language about being led to pray for our team. By the time I made it down to our late service in the theater, I had pretty much forgotten what I was going to preach and explained to the group that I felt we just needed to pray and worship God and that I would explain what was going on next week, after I had a little time to process what I had just experienced.

Just before leaving church to head home, I was stopped by Tim Bussell, a leader and mentor in our ministry. He explained that his son, Benji, who had been on a missions trip in Costa Rica during the time we were in Cambodia had felt that he should pray for us. He said that they were talking and Benji stopped mid-sentence and said they needed to pray for me.

When I asked Tim what day that that happened, he turned to his wife, Char, who said that she believed it was either Monday or Tuesday morning. Mind blown, I had to leave. I just looked at Tim and said that I needed to go home and be with my wife and family...and that I would explain what was going on later that week.

The power of what this all represented—within the scope of what was happening on the other side of the world—was astonishing. By now we had coined the term "Trash Mountain miracle of the day." This is what we began calling the unexplainable things—like multiple persons called to prayer at the exact moment we were facing the threat of death—that seemed to be happening on an almost-daily basis.

GOOD WORD: RESCUED BY PRAYER ~ DR. JIM CONGDON

Brett was experiencing the truth of the words: "The urgent request of a righteous person is very powerful in its effect" (James 5:16, HCSB). Stories from missionaries all over the world attest that the prayers of faithful, fervent believers back home accomplish wonders. One missionary wrote, "Unprayed for, I feel like a diver at the bottom of a river with no air to breathe, or like a fireman on a blazing building with an empty hose." You may not be able to go across the world, but you can pray. And it makes a difference. To paraphrase William Temple, renowned teacher, preacher, and Anglican bishop: When we pray, coincidences happen, and when we don't pray, they don't.

ANGEL SIGHTING?

It wasn't until several weeks later, one day before the release of the Cambodia documentary, that I noticed it. After leaving my position at the church, Michael was generous enough to allow me to set up a workstation at the Barrett Creative offices. I was sitting in front of my computer trying to lay out what we would say at the documentary premiere event the following evening. As I stared at the screensaver, it hit me. Could I possibly be seeing this right? Maybe I wasn't remembering everything accurately. I had written everything down in my notes throughout our journey in Cambodia, and, after reviewing them, I realized that the discrepancy I was seeing was for real.

Knowing that I wasn't the only person who was involved in taking that photo, and that if I was to be honest with myself and anyone I shared this story with, I needed a second opinion on what I was seeing. I went into Michael's office and asked him if he remembered helping me with the shutter speed on the camera so that I could capture that last picture of the truck coming down the road before it was completely dark that evening? He said, "Yes." I also confirmed that the main reason we wanted the picture was the man on top of the truck waiving and smiling at us. As I explained earlier, this was very unusual. He said, "Yes." I didn't want to show him the picture until I had asked this pertinent question so as not to lead him in his answer.

Michael went on to say that he remembered seeing two guys on top of the truck; I recalled seeing only one. The main point I was trying to confirm was that we both remembered seeing someone on top of the truck that even at the time seemed eerily out of place. In addition, I asked him if he remembered all of the guys in the cab of the truck who were all saying something chaotically to our interpreter, Sam, when it pulled up? He said, "Yes."

At that point, I felt that I had shown due diligence in questioning Michael's recollection of the event. I asked him to go to my computer and look at the screensaver, which I had already enlarged for further clarity. The photograph clearly showed that there was nobody on top of the truck—and that there was nobody in the cab of the truck, either, except the driver, of course. When the revelation of what actually took place that night hit us, Michael said nothing. He started shaking his head, walked into his office and shut the door. A few minutes later, he emerged from his office and said that he needed to go home and take a break to think about what had happened.

Interestingly, in the Gospel accounts found in Matthew and Mark, one angel was reported at the tomb of Jesus after His resurrection, but Luke and John report seeing two angels at the tomb. Not a claim that that was like the resurrection scene, or that we had 100% proof that what we had seen were actual angels, just an interesting parallel to an amazing divine intervention. If I had to pick, that night was one of the most moving and faith-building moments of my life. It was the most obvious time for me when the spiritual realm was touching earth in our midst. I had heard many pastors say that there are moments when we serve God's children that it is in a sense, heaven touching earth as a testament to His love for us. It was a clear example of God's providential move before us.

It is one thing for me to make a claim that I heard a voice that wasn't human in its origin. Or, that we had people praying on the other side of the world for our protection when we were delivered from the hands of murderers. Or that something had spooked the two guys that had followed us that night. Or that there were in fact people present in a situation, yet a picture showed otherwise. But when you add all of this up, and you take into account that there were multiple witnesses and multiple players involved in the account, what are the odds of this being anything less than what we believe it to be?

Chapter 8:

A KNOCK AT THE DOOR...
AGAIN

———•—•———

By the time I returned from Cambodia, my position at the church was winding down, and we were moving on with TMP. They generously allowed me to move my office out, even though I was technically still on staff at the church. The day I was moving into my new office at Barrett Creative, the mail came with a letter from the IRS. It was our approval letter for Trash Mountain Project's 501(c)3 tax-exempt status, received only weeks after we submitted the paperwork. We had been advised that the wait to receive our approval letter could be up to one year or longer. To get approval that quickly was just another confirmation of God's favor on what we were doing.

As we were going through the process of incorporation, I was wondering if churches were going to get on board with TMP. We really wanted to work through the local church, as we believe that it is the mechanism that Jesus put in place to spread His message. But who were we? We had not experience, and I was only 29-years-old at the time. We had one video and were about to release a second one, but we really weren't very organized yet. Little did we know that God was already working behind the scenes, making connections with the places and people that would form our future support structure.

Prior to leaving for Cambodia, on the day I went through the turmoil of being fired by the church, I went home and told my wife what had happened and had a long cry with her as we wondered how we were going to move forward with TMP. Later in the day, I was in my car, after picking up a bunch of computers donated for us to take to Cambodia, when I got a call from a friend. He said he was at a business luncheon in Lakeland, had talked with a girl who had already talked with her church: Ridgepoint Church in Winter Haven, Florida. They were interested in meeting with me about Trash Mountain. They saw the Honduras video and wanted to join us and see how we could partner together.

This was a big deal. We later met with them and their lead pastor, Timm Collins (who later became TMP's full-time Discipleship Director). They were the first church to embrace the TMP mission and vision. It was another confirmation. It was a difficult, but incredible time to see God moving in people around us, making things happen, and beginning the process of putting all of the pieces together to make TMP a reality.

Despite the continued confirmations and clear provision of God for our start-up needs, Jaelle and I were having a hard time figuring out our end of things financially. How were we going to make a living and take care of our growing family while we were trying to help others in much deeper need?

It was tough to even think about taking a salary to do something like TMP when the people we served were dying. But we had to function as a healthy family back home if we were ever going to make a difference overseas. We knew that it's just not going to work if the home base isn't strong. It is like when you are on a flight and they tell you to secure your own oxygen mask first before assisting others. This sounds kind of selfish when you first hear it, but now it seemed to make sense.

One evening I returned home from the office to find that Jaelle had had a very hard day. She explained that we were already carrying debt on our credit card. Our bank account was down to our last $7, and she needed to buy diapers and baby formula, but we didn't have the money. We had no savings and no safety net of any kind. And we didn't want to go to family or friends and ask for help. We needed God to move in the hearts of people to support us as missionaries.

Jaelle was in our bedroom crying and praying. The baby was crying, and life just sucked at that moment. So I began crying out to God. I prayed, *God, I am not comfortable asking You for help sometimes, especially when it comes to a request for money, and that is my fault, my own pride, and my imperfection, and I just have a hard time with it. But, we have invested our entire lives into this ministry, including our finances, so how do You expect me to effectively serve You when I can't even take care of my own family? I am failing as a husband and father. Help!*

I was petting and talking to my dog, Hank, sitting on my lap as I was praying. I said to him, "Buddy, we are going to get through this." Dogs are great. They just look at you with that absent-minded smile and not a care in the world. They don't ask anything, and they don't worry. As I was talking to Hank and praying, literally at my wit's end, there was a big bang on the door. It startled me because our couch backed up to the door and it was fairly late in the evening. I thought, *Hmmm, this is interesting.*

The porch screen door swung open really fast. I knew someone had knocked on the door and ran. I jumped up and chased after them. As I bolted out the gate (those who know me will get a laugh out of me using the word "bolted" to describe my speed), I saw feet going over some bushes in our neighbor's yard. I followed as quickly as I could, but whoever it was, was definitely faster than I was. I followed him as he jumped in a car, as I was hollering at him. The car sped off and I couldn't tell who it was. He had a hood on, and I didn't recognize the car.

Perplexed and a little amped up from the encounter I returned home. As I was about to walk inside, I kicked a little clay box lying on the ground. It looked like something someone had made in an art class. On the top of the box it said, "The Lord will fulfill His purpose for me..." (Psalm 138:8). I opened the box and looked inside to find a note on top of a pile of money. The note said, "Pressed down, shaken up, running over." It was a quote taken from Luke 6:38. Underneath it was a large pile of cash totaling one thousand dollars. We had not spoken to anyone about the financial burden we were feeling as we launched TMP—it was a God thing. I looked up at Jaelle who had come out of our room to see what was going on, and I handed it to her with tears in my eyes. I said, "I have no idea where this came from, but someone just left it on our porch." We broke down together, praying and crying and thanking God for His provision.

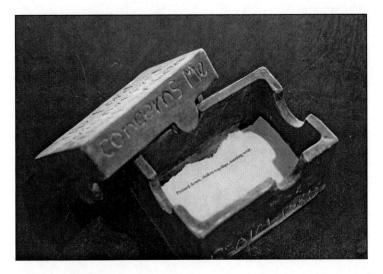

I have my suspicions, but no one has ever come clean with me. If you are reading this book, please know how eternally grateful we are for your generosity. If you didn't know that you were answering a prayer in real time, you know now. We started calling it our "angel on the porch."

The gift carried us through to a time when we could start drawing a small salary from TMP. The timing was just staggering—when my wife and I were asking God for help, He rescued us. When something like that happens, all you can do is say thank you, Jesus, for caring. There is nothing else we could say. It was just another reminder that He is in control and that this was His mission, not ours.

GOOD WORD: BIBLICAL COINCIDENCE ~ DR. JIM CONGDON

A coincidence is "a striking occurrence of two or more events at one time, apparently by mere chance" *(Source: Dictionary. com)*. The story of TMP is full of apparent coincidences. True, these are stories of how God moved in people's hearts to give generously to TMP, but they are also coincidences.

But what is a Christian to think about coincidence? If God is the Ruler of history, who "works all things after the counsel of His will" (Ephesians 1:11), can there be such a thing as chance, random events, and coincidences? It's a thorny issue, and how you come down on that issue is hooked into what you believe about huge issues like predestination, and providence, and God's control of the future. In my view the Bible and common sense drive us to four conclusions about coincidence:

1. On the one hand: Yes, the Bible says, there are coincidences, random events, and chance happenings.

     God tells us: "The race is not to the swift or the battle to the strong...but time and *chance* happen to them all" (Ecclesiastes 9:11). Elsewhere He says that "*By chance* Ruth entered the field of Boaz" (Ruth 2:3) and that "someone drew his bow *at random* and hit the king of Israel between the sections of his armor" (1 Kings 22:34). And Jesus, himself, telling the story of the Good Samaritan, said "*by chance* a priest was going down that road" (Luke 10:31).

So at the minimum, we can say that if we are too spiritual to allow Christians to use words like "chance" and "coincidence," then we are more spiritual than God!

2. At the same time: No, there is no such thing as a "mere coincidence," a totally random event due only to blind chance.

The Bible makes it clear that chance events and coincidences fall within God's plan and under His control. The writers of Ruth and 1 Kings make it clear that, while it seemed mere chance, God was the invisible cause who moved Ruth to enter the field of Boaz and the Syrian arrow to strike the king in the vulnerable spot of his armor.

To sum it up, God is sovereign, the all-wise, all-powerful Ruler of history. Before the world began, He chose a wise and benevolent plan for creation that would give Him glory (Isaiah 48:11; Ephesians 1:6). And because now He "works all things according to His will," nothing happens by "mere" chance. What appears to us as chance and coincidence is actually God's providence, His plan in operation.

3. Caution: God does not promise anyone the ability to "read coincidences" reliably.

Many people over-emphasize the importance of coincidences in their decision-making. Some people think that God is inaudibly revealing His will to those among us who are spiritually attuned enough to be able to read circumstances. But the Bible never suggests trying to read circumstances, nor do the biblical saints ever do it. Reading signs and stars was something that superstitious pagans did.

Coincidences are more like the Rorschach Test, the psychological test with big ink blots. Everyone sees the same blots, but not everyone sees the same thing. And how I read them sometimes tells more about me than it does about what God is saying.

4. Encouragement: This doesn't mean "coincidences" are unimportant.

Quite the contrary. To the Christian who knows that there are no "mere" coincidences in God's kingdom, coincidences are whispers from the Shepherd, "Just wanted to remind you that I am with you" (Psalm 23:4). They are surprise gifts from our secret Lover in heaven. They are nudges, "Shouldn't you spend more time with this person?" And they are sometimes tweaks on the ear: "Hey, your thinking is too small. Have you thought of this?"

AN OLD FRIEND

While we were grateful for God's provision through the one-time gift on the porch, we knew that we would need regular ongoing support to pay our family bills. We have a great network of family and friends, but we had never asked them for anything like this. We hadn't really talked with anyone about funding, because, based on the unusual and sometimes miraculous things we had witnessed at the start of this ministry, we felt convicted to leave it in God's hands and only ask when we absolutely had to.

I have an old friend, Shawn Potter, from my childhood in Topeka. I have known Shawn for as long as I can remember. I had the honor of officiating his wedding the previous summer—a beach wedding in Florida. It doesn't get much better. He definitely joined the "married over my head" club when God put Rosa in his life. I am a long-time member myself.

Shawn and Rosa were coming to Florida on vacation over the fourth of July, 2009. They wanted to visit the beach where they were married, and asked if Jaelle and I wanted to join them for a little time away. We really needed a break, so we took a day off and went over to the Sarasota area to meet them. As Jaelle and Rosa walked ahead of us to the beach, I asked Shawn how work was going, and he said, "Great." He is a mortgage broker, and I wasn't sure how things would be for him with the current economy. He asked how things were with us, as he knew I was leaving my job at the church. He had seen the Honduras documentary and wondered about our plans for TMP. I mentioned that I was done at the church in the middle of August and would be going full time with TMP on September 1.

As a businessman, he immediately questioned "How are you guys going to do this? Are you going to be like typical missionaries who need to raise money for your income?" We talked about it briefly, and I explained that we weren't really sure what the plan was. We were just starting to pray, asking God to provide. We were going to have to start meeting with people and churches, but for now, we were waiting on God. I could tell he was processing everything, but I didn't really think anything about it. Shawn was a person I would have talked to about support. But I hadn't planned on doing it that day, and I wasn't expecting the response he gave me.

We quickened our pace to catch up with our wives. Shawn snagged Rosa, walking away to talk for a few minutes. When he came back, he said, "We're in! We want to support you guys. We feel strongly about what you are doing in stepping out in faith to serve God in this way. We love you and Jaelle, and I will get back to you after vacation to see what we can do. We can set something up as a monthly gift starting in August."

I was in shock. This really caught me off guard. We were even more amazed when it came time to start his monthly gift, and Shawn gave me the amount. It was much more than we had expected, and hands down the most support we had even had anyone talk about with us. Our family's need for support was a big mountain to move, but Shawn and Rosa had just knocked out quite a large chunk of it. It was a huge encouragement.

Over the coming months and years, it seemed like each time my family had a specific need, like additional income or health insurance, God used the Potters to provide. The second example of such provision was when it came time to add a health insurance plan for TMP staff. We had gone on Cobra health insurance after losing my job with the church. Not a great option, but the only one we had. As an organization, TMP couldn't have any type of group insurance plan until we at least had a second employee. For my family, the clock was ticking. Cobra only lasts for so long.

In November 2010, our Board of Directors decided to hire Jon DeMeo as our new mission's director (more on Jon later). With a second employee, we could establish a group health insurance plan, and we knew it would increase our compensation package by $500 a month. However, I was nervous about whether we could afford this expense as a ministry. One morning I arrived at the TMP office just after learning how much the insurance was going to cost, and what I had raised for my missions support. We were going to be around $500 short of what we needed—just to stay at the salary we had been receiving and begin our health insurance. I was stressed.

I prayed about the need, left it in God's hands, and was not going to say anything to anybody. Just minutes later, I was driving away looking at my e-mail, (I know I shouldn't be doing that), and all I saw was the subject line "PayPal credit card?" It was from Shawn, and there was a question mark. I thought, *Oh no!* My mind went immediately to negative thinking, *He is not going to be able to support us for as much or he needs to change and make it lower or something has happened at work.* I was already nervous.

In my prayers that morning, I had requested provision for our health insurance needs. It was only the second time I had prayed specifically about money for my family's needs. But that time, I prayed to God with a specific request, *We need $500 more* *a month. My family has to have this, and the ministry has to have this group plan to move forward with more staff. We need to be able to offer health insurance and to do that I had to be concerned about the money. I need to be able to hold up my end in terms of fundraising for my own compensation package. Please help.*

I pulled up to a stoplight and opened the e-mail, and it said, "Please call me about my monthly gift as I want to increase it." I thought, *Are you kidding me? It's the opposite of what I had thought.* I excitedly called Shawn and said, "What's going on, I saw your e-mail. That's awesome. The timing is incredible. I'll have to tell you about it later. What do you want me to increase your monthly donation to?" You could probably guess what he raised it by. "Please raise it by $500," he replied. I nearly wrecked my car when he said it. Finding myself in tears (I cried a lot during this season of my life), I pulled over to process what had just happened, and to thank God for His provision.

About six months later, the ministry had a very specific need of several thousand dollars, and we had no idea where it was going to come from. It was for an overseas project, and it came up as we were leaving the country—and it was urgent. Shawn called when we were in the airport and told me he had been doing well at work and in addition to his monthly gift, he wanted to make a one-time donation. He said he would like to donate X amount, and it was to the dollar of what we needed for that specific project. I stopped him and asked if he was serious. I then told him what was going on. He was silent until he broke out in laughter and replied that that was awesome, that I was to use the gift to meet the urgent need.

Most recently, about a year after that first increase in monthly support from the Potters, we had another need come up for our family's support. There had been an increase in medical expenses. Jaelle and I had been blessed with our fourth child about eight months earlier. We had discussed needing a raise, but we had never requested it. We didn't know where the money would come from, and we didn't want it to come from TMP's general operations budget. We wanted to keep the same strategy for raising 100% of our personal support.

As a family, we had stretched all that we could. We went to our Board of Directors and said, "We are struggling and need to have an increase. I am not sure where it will come from, but we know God will provide." Our treasurer sent out a request, and that night the board approved a raise. Guess who texted me the very next morning, asking me to call him about his monthly support? So, I called Shawn, and he said he wanted to raise his monthly support once again—by $100 more than the board had just approved for my raise. So there was even some left over for the general operations budget. I started laughing and explained that he had done it again. He laughed and said that each time he had felt an unusual prompting to increase his giving.

This kind of thing has happened a few other times with the Potters, and we consider them to be our personal angels from above. It has been one of those ongoing, eerie–circumstances where he is being prompted as we are praying to do exactly what is needed. It is amazing to watch how Shawn and Rosa have paid attention to what is going on and have stayed sensitive to God's prompting—yet they had never been asked to support us with their generosity.

Chapter 9:

EXPANSION

———•—•———

B ecause Church at the Mall's children's ministry had raised
the money for our first two home-building projects in
Honduras, I was invited to be a part of their mission's event in
the fall of 2009. I was not necessarily comfortable with what
had happened with the church—I was still hurt by how things
transpired—so I was hesitant to attend. But I thought that since
they were willing to highlight the ministry of TMP and were
making an effort to move the church toward more missions'
involvement; I should be supportive, put my personal feelings
aside, and attend.

I showed up at the event by myself and took nothing with
me other than a few Honduras and Cambodia DVDs. When
I arrived, a mutual friend introduced me to a man from the
Dominican Republic, Roberto Rodriguez. Roberto had lived in
Lakeland for a number of years and had heard about what TMP
does and wanted to meet me.

Roberto had a friend in the Dominican Republic named
Pablo Ureña, founder of an organization called Niños con una
Esperanza (Kids With A Hope) in Santiago. He worked in an
area that seemed similar to the TMP documentaries of Honduras
and Cambodia he had seen. He explained that what Pablo was

doing seemed to fit with our ministry goals and wondered if we had considered expansion into a new country.

Roberto went on to tell me that Pablo was coming to Florida to talk to potential church partners and others about what he was doing, and would I be interested in talking with him. Roberto had told him about TMP and the documentaries, and he was excited about our mission. At the end of the evening, we made plans to meet with Pastor Ureña later that week.

Even though I hadn't wanted to go to the event, it had been worthwhile. I had a chance to meet Roberto. This contact led to what would become our largest and greatest focus ministry area in the world—so far. That was definitely one of those things that God put in place for the future of the ministry. It haunts me to think of what we would have missed out on if I had let my pride and personal feelings for the church get in the way and stayed home that night.

PASTOR PABLO

I talked with our board about meeting with Pablo and finding out what was going on with his ministry. We weren't specifically looking to expand, but we did need to know more about what was going on in the world of trash dump communities, where they are located, their similarities, and other such research.

Michael and I went to meet with Roberto, Pablo, and Pablo's' wife Elisabet. We enjoyed getting to hear his heart for what they did in the dump community in Santiago, Dominican Republic. They were in the same type of situation we had seen in Honduras and Cambodia. As we talked to Pablo, it became obvious that he was really stressed out. He had no American connection in terms of support on a regular basis like what we had seen in Honduras and Cambodia.

In Honduras, we knew that Amor Fe Esperanza had solid US-based ministry partners, such as World Gospel Mission. In Cambodia, we had decided to partner with People for Care and

Learning, a US-based ministry and Cambodian NGO. For Kids With A Hope, no one supported them, other than a handful of Spanish-speaking churches in Florida. There were a few churches and organizations that had taken teams down and a short-term grant from a foundation, but nothing much in the form of long-term, ongoing support.

The more we talked with Pablo, the more Michael and I knew that something felt right about that man, his heart, and his vision. After some words of encouragement and support, we told Pablo that it was great to meet him, and we would pray about his need and present it to our board. We shook hands and said that we would be in touch, explaining we felt this may be something God was leading us to but that we needed to take the time to discuss and pray about it.

PANERA BREAD ANGEL

After our meeting with Roberto and Pablo, we decided we really needed to go down to the Dominican Republic and see things firsthand. We didn't want to commit to anything, but knew that we needed to move forward with research and development within trash dump communities. We wanted to go, even if we were just to be an encouragement to Pablo. We knew that anyone leading a ministry of this type needs prayer partners. At the very least, we could be someone he could be in communication with here in the United States.

I set up a meeting with Roberto at Panera Bread. It is an easy place to find, and I often used it as an "office" because of the free Wi-Fi. One of my biggest concerns going into that meeting was that we didn't have the funds to travel to the Dominican Republic. We just knew that we were supposed to go. Michael had to stay home to focus on his business, so only Roberto and I could make the trip. But we only had enough money to cover one flight.

As I was praying about our financial restrictions and needs, I felt convicted that if we were going to have this man who had offered to go with us to translate, make connections, assist us with people on the ground, and introduce us to Pablo, we needed to at least offer to pay his way. I also knew that things were financially tight for him at the time—he was a real estate agent in the Florida market that had tanked. After praying, I had a real peace about the fact that God would provide for this need, I just didn't know how.

As we sat in Panera talking, looking at dates, and planning for a trip in February of 2010, I said, "Things are tight, but we want to cover your way. I know it would be a stretch for you, and since you are willing to take time off from work to come with us and be a translator who has a heart for God, we really want to be able to cover this." He said, "Wow! I was trying to figure out how I was going to do it, but I just knew God wanted me to go." We both laughed at the fact that we were both thinking similar thoughts and continued to talk about our plans.

As we were talking, a gentleman walked up to us and leaned into our table and said, "Excuse me. I don't want to sound like I was eavesdropping, but at some level I guess I was. My name is John, and I overheard you say something about missions or humanitarian work you were going to be doing in the Dominican Republic. Is that what you do?"

I replied in the affirmative and introduced myself. Roberto followed, introduced himself and said he was originally from the Dominican Republic. We wondered what John was getting at.

He said, "Are you going to be flying to Santo Domingo or Santiago?"

Roberto replied, "We need to be in Santiago, but we are just trying to figure that out now."

John said, "I know this may sound odd, but I felt like I was meant to come over here and offer you something."

We looked at each other, looked at him, and said, "What's that?"

He said, "I am a pilot for Jet Blue Airlines, and I have helped some people before with buddy passes to lower the cost of travel. As a pilot, I can give my buddy passes to whoever I want. So you guys could basically fly down to the Dominican Republic for the cost of taxes and fees, and that's it. There is no other charge."

Roberto and I looked at each other thinking, *didn't we just have a conversation about needing the money for this?* Then we looked up at him and then each other again.

John continued, "The weird thing is, I have never been to Lakeland before. Being a pilot, I fly out of Orlando and Tampa regularly, but there are times that I have to drive the I-4 corridor from Tampa to Orlando, which I was doing today. There was some big sinkhole on the highway and my GPS shot me off to a secondary route. I needed to check my e-mail and knew that Panera had free Wi-Fi, so I looked for the nearest location on their website, and it sent me here. That's the only reason I am here, so this is kind of unusual. We are all here at the same time, and I may be able to help you out with something. I'm sure that if you are a missions organization, dollars can be tight."

We were sitting there, trying to take it all in and thinking that it was too good to be true. However, it wasn't. For our first several trips into the Dominican Republic, John gave us buddy passes to help us out. It made it more than affordable for us to get down there, and really set the table for all that we did moving forward in the Dominican Republic. It actually ended up falling within budget for what it would cost one of us to go, but ended up covering both of us because of John's generosity. God's two-for-the-price-of-one deal!

THE HOLY SPIRIT DESCENDS ON A COFFEE MUG

My parents, as well as my brother and his family, have been attending Topeka Bible Church (TBC) since 2001. I met the lead pastor, Jim Congdon, two or three times when attending church with my family while on break from seminary or during the time that we lived in Florida. I always had a great deal of respect for him and had listened to his recorded messages many times. I knew that he was a well-respected pastor and biblical scholar.

Throughout the years, there were many times I felt a prompting to send him an e-mail of encouragement. I also prayed for him on a regular basis, even though I didn't really know him that well—something I hadn't done with anyone else who wasn't a good friend. I was prompted to pray for his leadership and that God would protect him and guide him as he led such an influential congregation in the Topeka area. Throughout that time, he heard about TMP, and I had sought him out for counsel a couple of times during the first several months of leading our new ministry.

Jaelle and I and the kids were planning to be in Topeka with my family for Christmas 2009, so I contacted Jim and we planned a meeting at Starbucks. I talked with him about TMP starting in Honduras and Cambodia, and the fact that we were beginning to look at launching a new work in the Dominican Republic.

Interestingly, the Lord had laid me and TMP on Jim's heart for a number of months. During this time, there were changes happening at Topeka Bible Church. For years, they had a two-pronged missions strategy: giving regular monthly support for several dozen missionaries and ministries, but also focusing major giving and development on one field project. A recent project building a Christian camp in the Philippines was ending, and Jim was asking the Lord what project was next. Jim had no idea that the Lord would speak to him that morning at Starbucks. As he says, God doesn't generally make His will crystal clear in a moment, and He'd never done it over a cup of java.

But, as we sipped our coffee, the moment that I said I was traveling to the Dominican Republic to investigate a trash dump community, Jim felt a tap on his heart, and a whisper. *That's it! That's TBC's next major missions project.* So convinced was he that this was the Holy Spirit that he blurted out, "Go to the

Dominican Republic, and check out Santiago. I really believe God wants this to be TBC's next major project." I looked at Jim, thinking, "This doesn't sound like you."

By the end of our time together, Jim laughed and said, "This is something that was supposed to happen." The entire conversation with Jim was another confirmation of our need to go investigate the possibilities in the Dominican Republic.

One of our biggest questions about the expansion of TMP concerned our capacity and which church partners and individuals we would plug into a new ministry location. And here was a partnership with Topeka Bible Church that was falling into place. Jim coined the saying about our meeting that "The Holy Spirit descended on our coffee mugs at Starbucks." I would have to agree with him, especially after hearing what was really going on inside of him during that meeting.

Since that initial meeting, Jim has become my pastor as I now attend Topeka Bible Church. On a more personal level, he has become a dear friend and mentor. Upon our return from the Dominican Republic, we shared with the church our vision for TMP and showed our Cambodia documentary as a visual example of what a trash dump community is and what it needs. This started a relationship with TBC that continues to this day. We look back on this as a God-ordained time for us and for the church. If they had not answered the call as a congregation to join us in partnership, I can't see how we would have moved forward in Santiago.

Currently, I live in Topeka and am co-authoring this book with Jim. He is actually the one who inspired me to write this book. I really only wanted to take on this project if he would be willing to team up with me. His heart for missions and the Church, along with his staggeringly clear understanding of God's Word, makes us a great team. Just one of these times, though, I want to win a debate with him concerning a biblical question. So far, I have not had the guts to jump in the ring with him.

It is fascinating to see how God can work through a relationship that for years was just based on prayer and encouragement of each other. Jim and I had no idea that we would be working together for God in any capacity. But God had our relationship in mind the whole time. It is another example of Him knowing what is in store, where we can look back and see in hindsight that this was something He was involved in from the start.

KIDS WITH A HOPE

At the beginning of 2010, we made our first trip to the Dominican Republic with Roberto Rodriguez. The dump community of Santiago was called Cienfuegos, which means "One Hundred Fires." This old landfill was surrounded by tens of thousands of people.

Pastor Pablo and his wife, Elisabet, let us know that they would be closing their doors soon if they could not secure ongoing financial support. There was a political leader who had committed a good amount of money in monthly support, but the checks stopped as soon as he was elected. They had counted on that support and knew if they did not have it their ministry could not continue. Beyond monthly support, the ministry had a debt that they had acquired trying to keep the doors open. The situation was so dire, that Pablo and his family were sacrificing by going without basic needs.

Pablo arranged for us to go up onto the dump. It was very typical of what we had seen before, with a lot of kids working, although not as many as we had seen in Honduras or Cambodia. That was mostly due to the fact that Kids With A Hope had contracted with the parents that if kids were part of the program, the kids would no longer go up on the dump.

While we were on the dump, Pablo saw one of the kids from his program. The child's dad ran after our vehicle and pleaded with Pablo not to discipline his child by kicking him out of the program. The dad assured Pablo that it wouldn't happen again and showed us that there was a real respect for and gratitude from the parents as far as their children being able to attend the program.

Up on the dump, we quickly realized that it was not a place where we were welcome. Anytime you go to a trash dump community as an outsider, especially with a camera, you see that there are a lot of people who don't want to be seen. It could be those running the dump or those working there. Within five minutes, I got hit in my face with a huge clod of dirt. Right after that, I was hit—right in the chest—with a large rock about the size of a softball. It actually knocked me to the ground. Next, a couple of bottles and some metal shards flew by my head.

I looked over at Roberto and Pablo and said, "Hey, we need to get out of here!" Pablo was so upset by the situation that he went over to talk with the gang of men responsible. I repeated that we needed to go. We dove into the truck and took off. We were able to get out of the area with only some bruised ribs and a few cuts. When we returned to the school, Pablo repeatedly apologized, but I said there was no reason for apology as that is the nature of what happens in the areas where we work.

As we walked around the community, we could tell that Pablo had a passion for the people, and especially for breaking the generational cycle that had affected the families for decades. I call it a generational cycle because in many dump communities families move to the community for one reason or another and then end up staying there for generations because it is all they know. Once they are locked into life in the dump there is very little hope of finding a livelihood outside of garbage. Pablo planned to break the cycle through the power of the Holy Spirit, and through giving the people the option of hope through education and encouragement. We instantly fell in love with Pablo, his family, and the entire staff at Kids With A Hope.

I explained to Pablo that we wouldn't commit to anything until we knew how God wanted us to move forward. Instantly, Pablo had tears in his eyes. It was obvious that our statement meant much to him. He went on to explain that he had been promised assistance many times by people within his own country, the Unites States, and other countries that had an emotional response to what was going on, but then never returned. I knew he understood that we wouldn't commit to something unless we could follow through.

It was during that first trip that Pablo introduced us to a man who ran the business on the property next to the school. You could see into this business from one of the classrooms at Kids With A Hope, and we became suspicious that he was running a sweatshop. We could see children and others working in horrible conditions, sewing and completing other tasks. The Kids With A Hope buildings were physically landlocked by this fool next door who had kids working like slaves making clothes.

My first impression of that man was that he was not a good person. I don't mean that in the typical sense. There was a cold darkness that was immediately present when we began talking with him. Pablo appeared nervous speaking with him, but told him that he wanted to move him away from his current location. The man had a house on the same piece of property. He asked him what it would cost to purchase his entire property and buildings and move him out of that area. The man asked way too much at first, but the price came down dramatically when Pablo turned the initial amount down.

Further discussion with Pablo confirmed our suspicions. We learned more of the despicable things the neighbor was doing with the kids and within the community. We realized it would take a move of God to provide the resources to stop the momentum he had in pulling the kids away from the trash dump to work in his sweatshop. That is when, after explaining the need to Topeka Bible Church, they gave us the money to move him out of the neighborhood. With TBC's support, a huge shift happened when we were able to buy those buildings.

Pablo's vision for Kids With A Hope included a nutrition program, health, dental and vision care, a technical school, and livelihood programs to help develop the ministry and surrounding community. Over time, we were able to install an industrial kitchen, a health clinic, classrooms, and storage on the new land, and greatly increased the school's capacity for meeting the need of the kids. God took a small geographic area that was clearly used for evil and turned it into good.

Chapter 10:

THE CHURCH RESPONDS

After meeting with Jim and sharing the TMP vision with Topeka Bible Church, there were some major things that happened almost simultaneously in the Dominican Republic as we committed to a partnership with Kids With A Hope.

I had sent a proposal that we buy the sweatshop next to the Kids With A Hope campus and cover the next several months of ongoing expenses for the ministry. We wanted this to include a salary for Pastor Pablo so that we knew his family was taken care of. We wanted to stop the financial bleed of a ministry that was doing such great work.

I was nervous as I sent the proposal because it was for a significant amount of money—around $45,000. I had requested an original amount and also the amount that they had already raised but were no longer using for the other overseas project. I received a response that they would provide that amount and even more. In the end, the church gave $50,000 to TMP for those specific needs and projects.

In many ways, the partnership and support from Topeka Bible Church launched the Dominican Republic project, which has now become the cornerstone of what we have done as a ministry over the past three years.

At the end of 2010, we were prompted to start a sponsorship program for the children attending Kids With A Hope. We had never done this before, but we needed to start a nutrition program for the kids as this was an urgent need. God provided Dr. Rick Tague, a physician from Topeka who attended Fellowship Bible Church, another church we have developed a partnership with and that has been monumental in our mission and the launch of Trash Mountain Dominican Republic. Dr. Tague and his family traveled with TMP to the Dominican Republic and saw the need to reverse the protein deficiency due to the kids eating minimal, and rarely nutritious, food. The families were unable to provide the necessary nutrition for their kids due to lack of resources. And if the kids had extra pesos, they were buying candy. Pastor Pablo had always wanted to start a nutrition program. When he talked about it, you could see his passion to meet this need. We agreed with him that we needed to move forward.

We didn't know much about sponsorship programs, but we did know that we wanted to do it a little differently. We didn't want to include any administrative fees in the sponsorship amounts enabling us to send 100% of the funds immediately to meet the urgent needs of the children. We also wanted to support the staff and teachers and get them to the level of pay that they needed to pay their bills and feed their own families.

The first Sunday we presented the new child sponsorship program at Topeka Bible Church, the number of people that committed to sponsorship—over 125—was staggering. I had talked with other ministries that said that they only got that kind of response at large conferences with a focus on a specific sponsorship program. They were shocked at the response we received. In the coming months, we had even more people sign up.

Fellowship Bible Church did a similar sponsorship drive a couple months later and we were able to sponsor most of the remaining 125 kids. We were now able to launch the feeding program and provide multivitamins to every child attending Kids With A Hope—250 kids! Fellowship Bible Church lead pastor, Joe Hishmeh, and the church were highly involved in mission outreach and made the decision to join in with TBC in the Trash Mountain Dominican Republic ministry. God was obviously using His global Church to respond to the need of His hurting children.

A CHEF ON A MISSION

We were in the process of finalizing plans to go to the Dominican Republic in December 2010 to construct a third story on the existing school building at Kids With A Hope. We were also going to transform the recently purchased sweat shop into a kitchen, health clinic, and outdoor cafeteria. We had a large team and had to close the trip to any more travelers from the two Topeka-based churches a few months before the trip.

Three weeks before our departure, I received an e-mail from Jim Congdon asking if a friend of his, Robert Krause, who really wanted to go on the trip, could come. Jim knew that we had already held the team meetings, and the trip was overloaded, but he thought his buddy should join our team. I responded that if this was someone he really wanted to come, and if he could afford to pay to get himself there, let's do it.

The very same morning that I received the e-mail from Jim, we realized that we had sponsored a lot of kids and would need to feed them starting the week of our trip. That meant cooking for over 250 children twice a day in a newly constructed kitchen with very limited equipment. Call it a brain fart on my part, but I had not planned for that aspect of our trip. I had only thought that if we had the money, we could provide the food. I had most definitely not thought that the reality of actually feeding 250 kids out of a small kitchen was beyond our experience and expertise.

I started to think if we knew anyone with kitchen experience who would know how to manage our nutrition program. Was there someone in the community we could hire to train the people in the Dominican Republic to cook? As we were planning for our final team meeting, I contacted Jim and asked about Robert Krause's skills. We had different teams doing medical and construction projects on the trip, and I wanted to find a good fit for Robert on one of the teams.

Jim told me, "Well I don't know what he can do. Maybe he can help with the Christmas party and meal you are planning to have for the kids."

He said, "Robert is a master chef and owns several restaurants and has a great amount of catering experience."

I about fell over on the floor when I heard that.

I said, "You have got to be kidding me. That is exactly what we have been praying about upon realizing that we needed to feed 250 kids every day. Would he be able to oversee and train the cooks we will hire?"

He said, "I am sure he would be up to the challenge."

Pablo had hired some Dominican women from the community to be cooks, but they were fairly intimidated by the ongoing task of feeding so many kids.

As soon as Robert arrived in the Dominican Republic, he started working with the women and learning more about the types of foods the kids were used to eating and what they liked, he began to prepare incredible meals that the kids gobbled up. He and his new team of cooks ended up bonding by the end of the trip. They were like their own little gang, complete with inside jokes. The women seemed to be in love with him, and they all wanted to know when he would be coming back.

After meeting with Dr. Tague, our nutritionist, to discuss nutritious and affordable ingredients available in Santiago, Robert ended up coming back several months later with more recipes he had developed after his first trip. He had another training session with the women that lasted several days, and the women became incredible cooks for the school. They were handling everything perfectly and transitioned to running the kitchen by January 2011. Through the sponsorship program and with God providing a chef out of nowhere, we were able to effectively launch the nutrition program.

I also started talking with Robert about catering special events back home, wondering if he had any experience with large-scale benefits. He had helped with many benefit events and said that he would love to offer his services free of charge to TMP for upcoming events. He said he could get great deals on food, much of which might even be donated, to provide the prep, and to do whatever was needed for our local events. That formed a partnership that led to our first major benefit event we called "Spoken."

In 2011 and 2012, Robert prepared a five-star meal for events of 320 and 740 people, respectively. He has been an integral part of what we are doing for the nutrition of the kids in the Dominican Republic and plans to go to the Philippines to train the cooks there. Who knew this guy who was led to join a trip late would become an irreplaceable part of our ministry.

ELDER CARE

In May 2011, we left for a trip to the Dominican Republic with plans to conduct a baseball clinic and complete some construction projects. Part of the team arrived on time. The rest of the team from Topeka had weather-related delays. There were numerous canceled flights, including one in St. Louis. The team that drove to St. Louis missed the flight, but got on one to Dallas. A normal 14 hours of travel time ended up being a 46-hour trip from Kansas City to the Dominican Republic.

I had to return to the United States to move my family from Florida to Kansas, and was scheduled to leave the Dominican Republic the morning they ended up arriving. I had read through the names of the team, and noted that an old friend, Cassidy McCrite, was on this trip. We had played on baseball teams together as kids, but really hadn't seen each other in over a decade. I just thought it was cool that he was coming to do a baseball clinic when that was the connection we had together years ago as children. Little did I know that God had very different plans for him.

When the team finally arrived at the hotel at around 2:00 AM, I greeted Cassidy and commented that we should get together and catch up some time back in Topeka. Since everyone was dog-tired, they went straight to bed, and I did not have time to say anything more to Cassidy. It's funny, and sad, how you have to go to a different country to reconnect with someone from your hometown.

One day, prior to Cassidy's arrival, Pablo pulled me aside to discuss a new need that he had been burdened by. He had an older gentleman he wanted me to meet. Pablo took me to a little apartment behind the school where this man was sitting alone in the doorway. You could tell by looking at his eyes that he was pretty much blind. He could barely walk. Pablo went on to tell me that there were some families who were struggling so hard to survive that they discarded their elderly family members. Since the elderly can't provide by working at the dump, they are often left to fend for themselves.

Pablo asked permission to feed this man from the food provided for the kids and if we cover the additional expense. Of course, that was a no-brainer decision. But it triggered me to ask how many others were in the same position as this man. I had always been so focused on kids that I had never thought about the needs of the elderly. The most vulnerable people in any community are usually the kids and the elderly—it's sad that I hadn't considered the second half of that equation until that moment. Pablo shared that there were quite a few elderly in need and that he would love to assist them. We agreed to begin to investigate some form of elder care ministry.

During the week following my return home, Pablo asked if a few people from the remaining team wanted to come with him when he went to feed the elderly man. At that point, no one remembered or knew what Cassidy's family did, but as soon as he heard "elderly man in need," he jumped to attention. Cassidy was very moved by that man and shared that his whole family was involved in the care of the elderly in the Topeka area. It was the passion of their entire family. It quickly became obvious to Cassidy what his ministry would be. He began to share with Pablo what could be done to help the elderly in the community. When the team returned to Topeka, I set up a meeting with Cassidy.

Cassidy shared how he had never felt God place him in a spot where his expertise and passion were so needed like He did in the Dominican Republic. The moment Pablo took him to see the elderly man, Cassidy felt moved to start investigating the possibility of elder care in the Dominican Republic and was excited about the different opportunities in front of him. He even started to draw up blueprints of how to provide a facility in the setting of the trash dump community.

The next summer, Cassidy invited his sister Katie, and her husband, Joe, on a trip to the Dominican Republic. McCrite Plaza, their family business, was our largest sponsor and provided a large portion of the food for our first Spoken event. Pat McCrite, Cassidy's father, was speechless after the event. A powerful, commanding man whose presence in a room is always noticed, I had never seen him like that before, and I was very moved by his response of support for TMP. The whole family is now involved and working on plans to continue their support of our new Elder Care Project.

THE SUMMER THAT CHANGED EVERYTHING

Through the summer of 2011, we had several trips to the Dominican Republic and Honduras that included building homes, fixing up the school, and adding kitchen facilities. The sponsorship program had really exploded, and we had a follow-up medical team going to provide checkups for the kids.

The teachers explained how the kids were completely different once the nutrition program started—more attentive, happy, expressive, and they appeared to be greatly improved physically. There was quite a difference in how the kids looked. Their eyes were brighter, their skin clearer, and they were more responsive and had more energy. There were also great spiritual and emotional changes. It was a wonderful provision of God, and the kids realized this. It was a tangible picture of God's hope and the difference that caring people could make in their lives.

There were multiple churches involved with the trips and projects that summer. TMP was beginning to become a neutral meeting ground for various churches to pull together and participate in the same ministry project. Secondary doctrinal issues were put aside, and we all worked together to build Christ's Kingdom. The one thing we all agreed on was the need to bring the Gospel message to trash dump communities.

This led to plans to start a Sunday morning church service in the Kids With A Hope facility at the end of that summer. They did a Wednesday night meeting in the area, but there were no established church or weekend services available. Pastor Pablo's desire was to add a weekend meeting, but it would have been too much on his already full plate. Pablo connected us with a man, who was hired to be the campus pastor for Kids With A Hope and to launch the new church. We planned to return in September to celebrate and worship with them for the first Sunday service. We had no idea that the journey we were about to embark on would change the entire course of our ministry.

Chapter 11:

OVERWHELMED

---•-•-•---

B efore sharing the story of what took place in September 2011, it is important that we backtrack a bit to explain the expansion of the ministry and the foundation back home which set the table for the story that was about to take place. After completing the Cambodia documentary, we partnered with Southeastern University in Lakeland, Florida, to do a documentary release premiere at the historic Polk Theater in downtown Lakeland in August 2009. As we were planning the event, we met with Hillary DeMeo, Student Life Director. I had worked with Hillary as a college pastor for the past few years.

During one conversation, Hillary mentioned that her brother-in-law had been on a mission trip to Cambodia with Southeastern and that it would be great to have a testimony from a student. He hadn't been over there with the TMP, but it was the same country and would show an interest in such missions from the student body. I thought it was a great idea, and so Jon DeMeo spoke at the opening of the event.

We had 1,400 people at the documentary's premiere and it built tremendous momentum for TMP. I didn't really have any interaction with Jon after that night except for seeing him on campus at Southeastern a couple of times. He basically fell off my radar.

Fast forward to November 2010 after I had been full time with TMP for a little over a year. I was having a hard time keeping up with the growth we were experiencing. Besides our Florida contacts, we had a lot of people in Kansas who were getting involved. I was being spread way too thin—working 80-hour weeks. Jaelle and I had dealt with so many trials throughout the foundation of TMP, and we were starting to buckle under the stress.

I told our board, "I know we can't afford to bring someone else on, I am not even fully funded yet, but we need somebody, or this thing is going to implode. This ministry can't move forward without someone else, because I am going to physically and mentally crack. In addition to the typical stresses of starting an organization or business, I am really having a hard time processing all of the horrors I have seen oversees and all that is riding on our shoulders in serving the people God has led us to. In addition, my family cannot handle this. My wife needs her husband back home, and my children need their father." It was a desperate plea for help. The board responded with great sympathy and agreed to pray about the need.

I had a friend in mind who I thought would be good for the position, but neither he nor I felt a peace about it. I wondered, *where do I start?* One morning I went to the office and told the Lord I couldn't handle leading by myself anymore. I prayed, "God, you have got to send someone, please. We need someone on staff that can shoulder this load with me. We have a ton of great volunteers and churches involved, but we need someone that will have a full-time vested interest in what is going on with TMP."

A couple of hours after I prayed that morning, I got an e-mail from Jon DeMeo. Even though I had many e-mails to respond to, I knew who he was and something told me to open his e-mail. He was graduating in December and had been loosely following TMP since the release of the Cambodia documentary. He said that he had a great respect for TMP and didn't know what he was going to do after graduation, other than getting married a few weeks later, and was inquiring about any possible job openings within our ministry.

Everything in me said *I don't know if this is the right choice.* He was young, and I had questions, but I decided that we would at least grab a cup of coffee. I wanted to hear his heart and his story and how he came to send me that e-mail. The timing of his e-mail was peculiar enough, or should I say God-timed enough, that I knew we at least needed to have a conversation.

We got together and after about two hours of talking I walked away thinking *this is the guy.* We couldn't have hit it off better, and he had so many of the skills and the heart we needed for missions. Jon knew he was supposed to be a missionary. He just wasn't sure if it was to be full-time on the field oversees, or with an organization here in the United States. He fit the part for the position we needed filled. In addition to his passion and experience with world missions, he was really good with graphic design and video, which is a huge part of what we do to tell our story.

It seemed like everything was falling into place as we talked. We were both very encouraged. I told him the situation with the ministry was not perfect. I didn't even know how we would pay him, but we would continue the conversation.

Within a couple of weeks, we had a board meeting, and I recommended Jon for the position without hesitation. Knowing that it was important for the second hire to be someone I liked and could work well with, I told the board that we needed to meet with him. I explained that the biggest hole they would see in his resume was not his experience, but his age. He was only 22 years old. He was just graduating college and would be getting married a month later. But I told the board that in my mind and heart this was the guy.

Jon, and his future wife Elaine, came to their interview with our board dressed to the nines. We were all laid-back in shorts and T-shirts. It was a somewhat intentional hazing, and we found that they both had quite a sense of humor about it, even though they felt a bit out of place. After an hour meeting, all of us looked at each other, and Dave Fleming said, "Is there any question?" Brent Nichols said the same thing and just started laughing. All of us agreed Jon was our guy.

We took a vote, which was a unanimous affirmation of who was going to be in the position of mission's director. Jon would be shouldering the load with me for all things TMP. At the conclusion of our meeting, Jaelle and I met Jon and Elaine at Starbucks. We said, "We are 100 % for you, and this job is yours. Here is how it will work: You are going to have to fund-raise as we can only guarantee a portion of your salary for a limited period of time. We don't know how to predict what is going to happen, so this is going to be a step of faith for you and for us." They said they were in, and wanted to move forward.

Over the next month, they got married and then came on staff. God answered our prayer to bring the right man—the right couple—into this ministry. Over the past several years, Jon has become one of my greatest friends, and is absolutely irreplaceable to what this ministry has been called to do.

THE TEAM GROWS

For Christmas 2010, my family and I stayed with my parents in Topeka. We were about to take a big team from Topeka to the Dominican Republic. We were in Topeka for a week and a half, and I met with about a dozen current and new supporters of TMP. I had several meetings with people I had never met before.

I called Jon from my parents' basement, standing by the fireplace (it was like one of those "Where were you when JFK was shot?" moments), and he started to ask questions regarding the financial need and plan. I said that we were not going to do the traditional "pass the plate" on Sunday. I told Jon that for his funding he should work with his network of people and let them know what he was doing. I made a broad statement about potential funding, "We have a lot of nets cast out there." Some of those nets felt like they were fairly significant.

Over the next three days, I met with Jim Congdon, who said the church had approved supporting my family financially at a significant level. Jaelle and I discussed how Shawn had come on board with help for our healthcare. And we knew what we would need for salary, which was no small amount of monthly support.

That meeting with Jim was the first I heard anything concerning Dennis and Gayla Greening. Jim said that we would love them and that he felt they were going to become a great blessing to the ministry. Oh how right he was!

Going to the Greening's home for dinner, Jaelle and I didn't know what to expect. As we talked that night, they shared they would like to support us and wondered what our biggest need was. Jaelle and I explained that we needed additional monthly support for my family as well as for the DeMeos. They shared the amount they would be giving and that the business where Dennis worked would match the amount, dollar for dollar. Dennis said, "If you want to use that amount for administrative needs, feel free to do that." The total was a large portion of the remainder that we needed for my family's support, and got Jon's family off to an incredible start.

Gayla mentioned some of her past work history and explained that she had always wanted to use her administrative skills to serve in a ministry. She said, "I wish I could help with something like Trash Mountain." I looked back and forth between Jaelle and Gayla and said, "I am so busy I feel like my head is about to explode. Have you seriously thought about serving in a ministry like ours? I am not an administrative detail-oriented kind of person and could really utilize someone with those skills." She thought I was joking at first, but when I said that there was a huge need for someone like her to join the team, she seemed to be thinking about it.

When Jaelle and I got in the car to leave, I asked her what she thought about having Gayla work in the TMP office. I had previously committed to our board that if I were to have an assistant working one-on-one with me, my wife would be the one to pick him or her. Jaelle developed an immediate love for Gayla and felt she would be a perfect fit for the position. We left the Greening's home feeling that God had just answered so many of our prayers from previous days. After bringing our official request to Gayla, she committed and informed us that she wanted to work voluntarily and not receive a salary, which she has continued to this day—now full time with TMP.

WE SOLD OUR HOUSE

The day after our dinner with the Greening family, I met with Chris and Carol Mammoliti. I had just caught wind of a story that a couple had sold their home so that they could give to TMP, but had no idea who these people were. The first time Chris and Carol heard me speak at Topeka Bible Church they were both really moved but did not share their feelings with each other. When they saw another presentation with the Cambodia video, they both were broken by God to join the TMP movement. After church, they said to each other that they had to get involved with this ministry. They didn't have the means to go on a trip or support TMP financially, so they looked to see where they could cut back to be able to help. They decided the only place they could make a cut would be their mortgage—and to do that, they would need to sell their home.

They had finally moved into their dream home, and never planned to leave, but to eventually spend their retirement years there. Even though the market was not great and their realtor said they would not get the best price, they wanted to move forward. They planned to do a few projects on the house before listing it, but received a call from the realtor with a prospective buyer. He showed the house and got an offer. The realtor said that though it was probably not the price that they had planned to list it for, it was still a good offer. In reality, the buyer offered more than they had planned to list the house for!

The Mammolitis quickly needed to find a house within a budget that would allow them to support TMP financially and be able to go on a mission trip to the Dominican Republic. They found a house, made a low offer, the seller accepted, and that brought them within two dollars of the monthly budget amount needed for all they had prayed about!

It was such an encouragement to see the faith of this couple, who had only heard a couple of group presentations on TMP, move forward with what they knew God would have them do. Just weeks after selling their home, Chris got a job with a new company at a higher salary. He also had paid vacation time, which enabled him and Carol to go on a mission trip with TMP. They had originally decided to financially support our administrative needs and forgo the trip, even though that is what they really wanted to do. Getting this new job and the benefits allowed them to sign on.

What's more, Chris is a biologist who has extensive experience as a fishery expert. I was interested in his work in aquaculture, as our board had been discussing the possibility of launching an aquaponics program to aid in self-sustainability within our international communities. Years later, we hired Chris to be our Director of Aquaponics. God worked out the details to give this faithful couple the desire that He had laid on their hearts, and only He knows what will happen next with this incredible family.

About 12 hours after meeting the Mammolitis, I received multiple calls from my brother and several others who wished to join the TMP financial support team. It was a landslide of support, and an answer to prayer that only God could have pulled off. The evening after having lunch with the Mammolitis, we received the biggest donation we had ever received from a donor I had never met. This all happened in a 72-hour period after telling Jon we had some "nets out." In a matter of hours, God had guided His people to sacrifice at a level that more than doubled our administrative budget and gave us a multitude of people who would become an integral part of our staff and team.

As if this wasn't enough, during this same 72-hour period, 24 hours before leaving with our team for the Dominican Republic, Roberto (the man who introduced me to Pablo and did all of our interpretation on our trips), had to back out on the trip due to commitments at work. We were stuck in a bad place with just one day to figure out what to do. It just so happens that a woman named Shelley Setchell had spoken to me at church just hours before learning about Roberto's unfortunate change of plans. She explained that she used to be a missionary in Mexico and was at the time a Spanish teacher at Cair Paravel-Latin School in Topeka (funny side note—I was expelled from that same school in the fifth grade, at no fault of my own…really).

Shelley went on to tell me that she was frustrated because she had tried to get on our first two teams to the Dominican Republic, but the teams had filled up too fast. When I received the call from Roberto, I had no idea what we were going to do, and then it clicked—what about that woman I met at church that morning? Would she be able to come on such short notice? I called her, and extended the invitation and she quickly made plans to come. Fortunately for us, her boss at the school was Mel Congdon, Pastor Jim's wife—go figure. Just 24 hours later, Shelley came on our trip and absolutely blew us all away with her ability to lead a team and translate. That trip started a process that led to her becoming a full-time missionary with TMP as our Latin America Missions Director just two years later.

It ended up being quite an astounding trip to Topeka that moved a lot of things forward in the ministry. It is encouraging to see how God can change everything and answer prayers in a matter of hours—at the very moment you feel you have reached your breaking point. This has been a continual pattern throughout the life of TMP, and it would take an entire book in and of itself to document all similar stories to the ones I just shared. It has been an incredible lesson in faith and learning more every day that we have been built to live in community with each other—and that there is order to everyone and everything that happens when following our Heavenly Father. This fact was about to be proven in ways that we could have never imagined.

Chapter 12:

A LITTLE GIRL IS SAVED

------·•·------

During our initial trip to the Dominican Republic in February 2010, Pablo had told us about a nine-year-old girl, Jeni, who was born HIV-positive. At her current stage of the disease, she was starting to struggle deeply with fighting infection and illness. The last few hours we were in country, I mentioned that I wanted to meet the girl with AIDS I had heard about.

Roberto interpreted for us, asking Jeni how she was feeling and whether there was anything we could do for her. We basically wanted to hear what was going on with her. She said something in reply to Roberto's questions, but, during a short pause, Roberto didn't translate—he was crying. When he regained his composure, he told us her reply, "I am sick. I've never felt good in my life. You are a pastor from the United States. If you have medicine that can make me feel good, can you bring some back for me?"

My heart exploded inside my chest. I've always had a rule to not commit to anything until we are sure we can help. But my response to Jeni just jumped out of my mouth. I said that I would do everything I could to help her and hopefully bring some medicine back for her. Deep down, I felt that there was something special about this girl, and that the Holy Spirit was leading me to respond in this way. I was thoroughly convinced that God was going to do something through her life. We left Jeni and the Dominican Republic later that day, fully intending to help her in any way possible.

After returning from that trip, Jeni's health began weighing heavily on my heart. For the first couple weeks home, something was prompting me about her every time I prayed. I wasn't sure what was going on, so I sent an e-mail to Pablo. He replied that she was actually very sick and had been in the hospital for the past week. They were not sure what to do because the hospital she was going to was not equipped to properly care for someone in her condition. It was an over-loaded free clinic and not a lot was getting done to help with long-term care or prevention with the proper medications. After learning this, we decided to send an SOS e-mail to our entire contact list to get people praying, and to hopefully find someone who had an idea of how to help her.

I contacted Connie Fleming, who was the TMP healthcare director at the time, and she told us that we needed to get a copy of Jeni's file so that she could share it with some specialists in HIV/AIDS care. Within 24 hours of sending the e-mail, we had received numerous responses, including a doctor in the Dominican Republic who then contacted someone else who connected us with a clinic that offered to take care of Jeni. They said that if we had an AIDS patient from a low-income family, their clinic was the place to come. We had no direct connection with this person, but through multiple people forwarding e-mails, the next thing we knew, they had a place for her—and all we had to do was provide the transportation to get her there. They were even going to cover the cost of all her meds and everything she needed to try and get her back on her feet.

It was quite an unusual deal to get connected with someone from the Dominican Republic who could help her so quickly. We rushed Jeni over to the clinic as quickly as we could. She received some of the proper medication that she had needed for years and started to recover. Over the next several weeks, there was daily improvement. The right medication was able to help fight off the infection. She started gaining weight, even though she could not eat all she needed to be healthy. Within a month, she was feeling much better! The medication was helping slow the progression of the disease, although we knew that she was far enough along that there was no way to completely reverse the process. God had quickly answered the prayers of his people to save this little girl.

DEVASTATED

During our September 2011 trip to launch the new church, Pablo, who knew that we had a vested interest in Jeni, told us she had been in the hospital for a few days and was not doing well. He thought we should go see her.

Our hearts immediately sank. We did not know what to do other than go check out the situation and pray. After leaving Pablo's house, I texted Jim Congdon, Joe Hishmeh, and my brother Derek requesting prayer and letting them know I was personally having a deep struggle with the news. Jeni had become like a daughter to me over the past year, and that update just crushed me.

When we arrived at the hospital, we found out she had been hospitalized due to an infection in her upper arm and also in her leg. Due to how progressed the AIDS infection was within her body, she was not responding to the medication anymore. The only possible outcomes and prognosis were bleak. We found her pale and emaciated, lying in the hospital bed barely moving. It did not look like she could even walk. They were trying to get her to sit up a little but it was difficult.

The hospital was like a horror movie: Blood on the floors, patients holding up their own IV bottles due to the lack of proper equipment. And, Jeni was in a room with other kids who had the flu and other airborne illnesses. Upon entering her room, we instantly saw her mom trying to be strong and hold back the tears. The head nurse told us if her body did not fight off this newest infection, she could die at any moment. Knowing that this was just one opinion, I couldn't bring myself to believe it. Standing there, holding my wife's hand on one side, and Jeni's on the other, I was screaming inside. But I couldn't let her see that.

Just before we left, she mustered up a smile and said, "I love you. Please come back and visit me." The air felt like it was sucked out of the room as I heard her kind words. Her mom followed us into the hall and broke down and explained that she was willing to do anything for her daughter, even send her to the United States if that was what was best for her. We agreed to meet the next day to discuss the options and walked away.

Those of us visiting Jeni that day left with a very bad feeling not knowing if she was going to make it out of that hospital and stay alive. We realized there just wasn't a whole lot we could do. The disease was running its course. The medications had slowed the inevitable, but eventually the disease would take her, and the doctors didn't think it was going to be long. We knew that this was coming, but we did not expect it to happen so soon.

Jon and I had a very hard time watching our wives process all that was taking place in front of us. Both Jaelle and Elaine are filled with such compassion and love for children, and Jaelle was actually pregnant with our fourth child. Words cannot describe the hopelessness that all of us were experiencing as we drove away.

When we arrived back at the hotel that night, I had a spiritual war going on inside of me. I asked Jaelle to go down to dinner ahead of me and said that I would follow in 10 to 15 minutes. As soon as she left the room, I broke down before God. I was angry at the situation and was crying out for His help and guidance. Why had He stepped in before when she needed His help if she was just going to end up in the same place again a year later? You know the kind of prayers where you say, what can WE do? Just show us, and WE will do it! Then my focus started turning more on me, and I saw the hypocrisy and lack of faith within my own life. I started talking to myself and thinking, *Why is it that when we pray we do not pray with the deep seeded faith that we know God can in fact do the impossible? I have sure talked a big game, and can preach it to others, but where was my faith?...*I felt as though I was failing God *and* this child.

In the modern American Church, it is unusual for us to see God physically heal someone. And we have seen the ministry of healing faked so many times by frauds that have infiltrated the Church that many Christians just don't think physical healing can happen anymore. Or, our churches teach that such things—healings—only happened with Jesus and the Disciples. I agree that there was a unique and one-time anointing on the Apostles, but where did Jesus or Paul or anyone teach us that He was going to leave us and not continue to be God on the earth?

As I finished pouring my heart out to the Lord, my mind flashed back to the passage God so clearly spoke to me in Cambodia, John 14. He said He would send the Holy Spirit and He would do greater things than had been seen through Jesus, Himself, and that He would not leave us as orphans. If He chose to reveal that to me in such a blatant and supernatural way two years before, wouldn't that apply to all of us as His followers today? And, if it applied to us today—why wouldn't it also apply in this moment, with this child?

AN IMPOSSIBLE PRAYER

Over dinner that night, Jaelle, Jon, Elaine, Roberto, and I discussed what we had seen in the hospital, what we could do, and talked about prayer. After the meal, I went back up to the room with Jaelle, shared my heart with her, and she motivated me even more to move. My wife is wonderfully blunt with me, and she basically told me to stop talking a big game and ACT. Her statement was eerily similar to what I had just prayed an hour before. I told Jaelle she was right and that I needed to go take care of something. I found Jon, and we went outside for a walk in front of the hotel. He was in the exact same state of mind that I was. We had to pray a bold and seemingly impossible prayer that God would heal Jeni. And we had to ask others to join us praying that we KNOW He can do this and that He WILL do this.

It's a dilemma, because we know that God's will IS God's will, and He is going to do what He is going to do, and it is perfect. We all need to be okay with and submit to and embrace that and know that He is in control of all things. But, on the flip side, I believe there is something to be said that we many times use the "His will be done" part of our prayer as a personal safety net. Honestly, I often say "your will be done" because I don't want to be let down when someone isn't healed, or I don't see God respond to my prayers in the way that I hoped.

So we decided that night at about 11:00 to send out a raw and uncut plea for prayer to everyone on our contact list via video. We set up in Jon's room and in one take said, "Hey this is what is going on," and I made a plea to our TMP family, explaining "from what we were just told, this little girl that many of us have gotten to know over the past year-and-a-half is going to die without God's healing touch. Period. There is nothing else that is going to halt this or slow it down. We really need everyone to be on this."

Jon was able to set up a website where people could sign up for one-hour prayer segments. On September 7, 2011, we launched a 24-hour, seven-day prayer for Jeni. We believed God was her only hope, and we would see Him move. We received a global response with e-mails and Facebook responses from people in different countries saying they were praying for Jeni. We started seeing the list grow longer of those signing up to pray.

Everyone was taking slots for prayer, and some people took multiple slots each day. Some signed up for 4:00 in the morning, 3:00 in the morning–those tougher times. They would get up for an hour and pray for our friend. They would commune with God and put Jeni's needs at His altar. We were all, as a community, counting on Him for this; she was counting on Him for this. There was no other hope.

After an amazing celebration Sunday establishing a new church, Jaelle and I sat down with Jeni's mother and father to talk about her options. After discussing her condition and making sure that we were all on the same page, the conversation took an emotional turn.

The two moms in the room took over. Jaelle turned to Jeni's mother and explained that she loved her daughter and would do anything she could to help her from our home in the United States. She welcomed the two of them into our home, explaining that there is an incredible children's hospital in Kansas City that would be able to offer Jeni the best care possible. Jaelle explained that the last thing we wanted to do was to take Jeni away from her family and home, but that Jeni's options seemed to be running out.

The tears began to flow, and as I was becoming overwhelmed, I locked eyes with Jeni's father and we shared a look that needed no translation or words at all. I had never seen him show any emotion as I believe he was trying to be a strong husband and father, but, in that moment, tears filled his eyes, and without words his eyes told me that he trusted me, even with his daughter. Overwhelmed, I gave him a hug, we shook hands, and he said thank you.

We left the Dominican Republic with heavy hearts, but also with a confidence that we were about to witness God move in the life of our little sister. We returned home a couple of days before the official launch time of the prayer. Soon after our return, I received a call from Pablo. Jeni's doctors had just told him that there wasn't a whole lot of hope for her. We were all desperate for God's intervention.

TWO DOCTORS EMERGE

Through someone who forwarded our e-mail plea on behalf of Jeni, we were introduced to Drs. Francisco and Diane Sabado. They are based out of Santo Domingo and work with hospice patients, including AIDS patients who are in the latter stages of the disease. It was only a couple hours' drive for the Sabados from Santo Domingo to Jeni's hospital in Santiago.

After e-mailing back and forth with the Sabados, Diane called me. She said they would love to meet Jeni and see if there was anything they could do to help with her care. She wanted to know if they could see her file or talk with her doctors to see if and how they could possibly offer their services. This was great because we now had someone from the medical community on the ground we could talk to since it was difficult to get ahold of anyone at the understaffed and overworked hospital. Not only that, but this was exactly the kind of thing they specialized in. We immediately put them in touch with Pablo and her hospital.

The next day, I received another call from Diane, and her news quickly crushed my optimism about the situation. She said, "This doesn't look good. Jeni's CD4 count is really low, her viral load is very high, and she may only have a few days. At best, maybe a couple of months if she can beat this infection, and that is being very optimistic. It will most likely only be days. If you want to say goodbye to your friend, you need to come back down, and soon." My heart sank. I stood in my driveway, looking up and thinking, *What is going on!?* I was overcome by desperation about the whole situation.

Then, almost immediately after I hung up with Diane, I received a call from Connie Fleming. She had talked to someone who gave her similar news based on Jeni's numbers. Connie said, "Brett, this isn't good. It does not look like there is a whole lot of time."

When I walked into the house after having those two conversations in the driveway that evening, Jaelle could see how torn up I was. After sharing what I had just learned, she said I had to go back to be with Jeni, and to stay as long as I needed. Everyone agreed that Jon and I should be with Jeni physically, praying for her and supporting her family until the end. We booked a flight to go back down the following Sunday. We decided that this was probably the last time we would see Jeni alive—and that was if the inevitable had not already taken place by the time we arrived.

HEAVEN TOUCHES EARTH

Thursday evening, just two days after deciding to return to the Dominican Republic, I received a call from the Sabados. They said they were planning to travel to Santiago and see Jeni the next morning to evaluate her condition and to help with formulating options for her care. That was about 36 hours after the 24/7 prayer had started. They said they had looked at Jeni's file but wanted to talk with her doctors in person, see her, and decide if there was anything they could do to help, even if just to treat her as they do many of their hospice patients. It was over. I had lost hope, and I was preparing for a very sad trip.

Then, the next morning I received a phone call from Diane Sabado—probably the most shocking and beautiful phone call I have ever answered. She said, "I am here with Jeni, and I have to say that this is not what we expected. She is bouncing off the walls. She is running around. She is playing. She's out of bed. She is eating. We have to tell her to calm down so she doesn't make herself worse. She has so much energy. We were expecting to see a girl with all the symptoms of the final stages of AIDS unable to even interact with people effectively. There is something different. I am not looking at a little girl with AIDS. All the symptoms they said she had when she went to bed last night are gone!"

Shocked, I said, "Please educate me like I am a child concerning HIV/AIDS because I am having a hard time following you. What are you telling me?"

She replied, "With AIDS, there are the numbers—the viral count and the CD4 count that is one thing—and then there are several physical symptoms that are typically present at this stage in the disease. Her doctor said she had all the physical symptoms, but they are all gone. And it happened overnight from what it looks like. She woke up today feeling better than she has for as far back as her mother can remember. The infections in her leg and upper arm and the other AIDS-related symptoms simply disappeared overnight."

I remember hanging up the phone in utter amazement and thinking, *What just happened? What did I just hear?* Leave it to me, the king of stubborn faith to question what just happened.

Jon and I kept our tickets to the Dominican Republic after deciding that we still needed to go. There is a big part of us that doesn't believe something until we see it, and, especially when dealing with a language barrier, we didn't want to jump ahead and report something had happened that was not accurate. We sent another e-mail out to the prayer team saying that we needed to keep the seven days of prayer going and that we were going to the Dominican Republic to see what had actually happened and report back. We told the prayer team to be encouraged, that something had happened.

GOOD WORD: PRAYING WITH CONFIDENCE ~ DR. JIM CONGDON

Brett has expressed succinctly the dilemma at the heart of intercessory prayer: we are to pray with boldness and confidence that God will give us what we ask for, and yet we are to pray with humility and submission because He may not.

And it is easy to fall off on one side or the other. On the one side, Mr. Over-confident prays with a Power Faith, saying: "I'm naming it, claiming it, and telling God what He must do." But this positions God as my servant. It also treats prayer as magic, a bit like Charlie Brown's famous "If you hold your hands upside-down, you get the opposite of what you pray for."

C.S. Lewis explains in *The Efficacy of Prayer*: "Prayer is request. The essence of request, as distinct from compulsion, is that it may or may not be granted. And if an infinitely wise Being listens to the requests of finite and foolish creatures, of course He will sometimes grant and sometimes refuse them." And he adds: "There are, no doubt, passages in the New Testament which may seem at first sight to promise an invariable granting of our prayers. But that cannot be what they really mean. For in the very heart of the story we meet a glaring instance to the contrary. In Gethsemane the holiest of all petitioners prayed three times that a certain cup might pass from Him. It did not. After that the idea that prayer is recommended to us as a sort of infallible gimmick may be dismissed."

Surely the Oxford professor was right. God is not my servant and prayer is not magic. So to banish the words "if it be Thy will" from our prayers in order to make sure we get what we want is to part ways with Jesus Himself and to try to manipulate God.

Too far on the other side, Miss No-Confidence prays with a Slot Machine Faith: "It won't cost me too much and I might hit the jackpot." With Brett, we must confess that at times we lack confidence in God, and so we "say 'your will be done' because [we] don't want to be let down when someone isn't healed." But for Jesus, "if it be Your will" was not a safety net or an add-on, but the heart of the prayer itself, a declaration of loving trust in the Father who knows best. In fact, our Father commands us to come into His presence with confidence, because we are His beloved children (Hebrews 4:16). Do you lack confidence? Remind yourself that prayer is not the overcoming of God's reluctance, but simply bringing your will into conformity with His will, so that He can righteously grant our requests (Stephen Olford).

So how do you pray when you want something desperately? First, make sure you are right with God, not cherishing sin in your heart (Psalm 66:18). Then march boldly into the Throne Room, come right up to your Father, and ask boldly for exactly what you want. Assure Him that of course you want exactly what He wants, because you know He knows best; but you know He loves to give His children the desires of their hearts, "so Lord, this is what I really want!" When hundreds of us did just that, saying "Lord, PLEASE heal Jeni, in Your will and for Your glory," He did!

TRANSFORMED

When Jon and I arrived in the Dominican Republic, we received a report from the doctor saying that Jeni was going to be released from the hospital that day. We met her at the clinic where they were drawing some blood to check her numbers— still trying to figure out what was going on, because none of what transpired was medically logical or even possible.

At the medical lab, we met the Sabados for the first time. They were also in shock. They shook their heads, saying they had never seen that disease at that stage of development where someone rebounded overnight. They said that just doesn't happen—and they work with patients like Jeni all the time.

We took the Sabados, Jeni, and her mom out for lunch. To that day, I had only seen her eat a bite or two of food at any given meal. She was usually struggling with her appetite and a great deal of nausea from her medication. But today, she horsed down a sandwich-and-a-half. She was laughing, doing pull ups on my arm, dancing, and running around. There was an image of true joy on her face. You could see that she felt better. Life was better. She knew things had improved. She was too young to understand the extent of her illness, yet she knew she had been sick for her entire life, and she knew she felt different that day.

A few months after all of that happened with Jeni, we received blood work back confirming that her numbers had improved dramatically with no explanation. She was still technically HIV-positive, just not in the AIDS stage of the disease anymore. The disease had simply reversed its progression. I asked the Sabados to explain that to me again because I was having trouble coming to grips with what all that this meant medically. Diane repeated that there are a set of symptoms that come with the disease at the AIDS stage. Her skin, her eyes, and every physical symptom that accompanies the blood numbers to diagnose a patient as having AIDS had disappeared overnight. The only thing Diane could say was that she believed God had healed that little girl.

In Jeni, the AIDS had reverted back to HIV, and her physical evaluation and how she was acting confirmed that. Everything was better. Now, we wish that she was free of HIV, but things had gone through the roof in terms of her numbers and her day-to-day life. And, according to her doctors, if we keep her on the right medications, she could live another 30 years or longer.

During a 48-hour period, Jeni went from hours, days, weeks, or at best a month or two to live, and now we were being told that if she has the proper care, and nutrition and keeps progressing as she is, she is going to be fine and live a fairly normal life. We were in awe! There was no way to respond to this other than to say "thank you God. You have saved Jeni. Your power and response to the prayer of your people has won the day once again!" The scary thing, though, is that the story did not end there. There was a much bigger thing happening right before us, but God had not granted us the eyes to see it. The table had been set for God to move far beyond the healing of one child in the Dominican Republic.

Chapter 13:

STAY

"And Jesus answered, "O faithless and twisted generation, how long am I to be with you? How long am I to bear with you? Bring him here to me." And Jesus rebuked him, and the demon came out of him, and the boy was healed instantly. Then the disciples came to Jesus privately and said, "Why could we not cast it out?" He said to them, "Because of your little faith. For truly, I say to you, if you have faith like a grain of mustard seed, you will say to this mountain, 'Move from here to there,' and it will move, and nothing will be impossible for you." (Matthew 17:17-20)

Since the foundation of Trash Mountain Project, the Philippines trash dump community problems have been on our radar and prayer screen. Our translator in Cambodia in 2009 was from the Philippines and had told me about the horrendous trash dump situation there. And, over the years, I had received several e-mails from Filipino missionaries asking if we had ever considered coming to their country to evaluate what was going on within their trash dump communities. But we had never felt any confirmation from God that we were to pursue any kind of work there.

Around the same time as Jeni's miracle, we had felt a strong leading to go to Bogota, Columbia, but it seemed that every time a door would seemingly open to go there, it would abruptly shut. At that point in the life of Trash Mountain, we had learned to pay attention to such things and to not discount anything as simply coincidence. I had even been open about the fact that the word coincidence had become a cuss word to me.

Then, to our surprise, during a conversation with Dr. Francisco Sabado, we were explaining the mission of Trash Mountain Project. He had posed a question concerning which countries we currently worked in and how we decide to move into a new location. I mentioned our leaning towards Columbia and possibly Mexico, but that for some reason of late I had developed a great burden for the Philippines through what I believed was God's guidance. Upon mentioning our prayer for the Philippines, his eyes lit up. We discovered that he had grown up there and had moved to the Dominican Republic about 20 years ago.

After meeting Dr. Fran through such unusual circumstances, we just figured that he and Diane would become great ministry partners within the Dominican Republic. We had never had in-country doctors who were on board with our mission, and we knew that this would be a huge benefit to the ministry. But, as Fran heard that we had been praying about the Philippines for a couple of years, he explained that he had a heart to go back and serve the poor within his home country, but he had never had the opportunity to do so. He said that this burden had greatly intensified in recent days.

The concept of helping people living and working in trash dumps was strong on his heart. It was born in him—we learned that he had even eaten out of the trash to survive when he was a child. He was brought to tears when describing his experience and hunger to give back to his home country—specifically to children facing the same trials he had faced in his own childhood. During that conversation with Fran, we looked at each other and thought that it seemed a little too perfect to not pursue. Fran could travel with us to research and investigate what was going on in the Philippines, and share his contacts on the ground, while providing medical care for those living in the Manila area dump communities.

Within the same week that we had the revelation with Fran, I received an e-mail from Ken Vander Hart, one of our board members, about a missionary who had been in Manila for almost two decades. Two of Ken's long-time friends had known of Jeff Long for some time and understood that he specializes in providing missions housing—so he can house teams—and is a well-connected guy with a heart for the Filipino people. We contacted Jeff, and he immediately offered to put us up in missions housing and to handle all the research that needed to be done on the dumps in Manila before we arrived on the ground.

Jeff was clear to point out that Manila is one of the biggest cities in the world with an estimated population of 12 million, and it would take someone who really knew the area to help us accomplish our goals in researching the landfills surrounding the city. He and his people started mapping out four different trash dump communities within the Metro Manila region. In just a matter of weeks, we had more logistics set up for a trip than we had ever had with any other location we visited. We could go and survey the situation within four dump communities in one city. With so many arrows seemingly pointing towards the Philippines, the decision was made to make the trip. Fran was on board with us to go and research the areas and also hold medical clinics in each of the four communities. So, on May 12, 2012, Jon, Fran, and me loaded up several duffel bags full of medical supplies and made the journey to Metro Manila.

After clearing customs, we exited the airport, immediately spotted Jeff and loaded our equipment and bags and ourselves into his van. After initial introductions, Jeff's first question was whether we were ready to work. We had just come off of 26 hours of travel, and it was 9:00 in the morning in Manila (a 13-hour time difference from home), but we said, "Yeah, sure! What have you got for us?"

SMOKEY MOUNTAIN

We went directly from the airport to our first research location at the Smokey Mountain/Pier 17 trash dump community. Arriving, we walked up to a small church that had a couple of hundred kids lined up waiting for medical treatment. Once Fran got the health clinic organized, Jon and I were taken on a tour of the community by the church's leader, Pastor Reynixon.

Smoky Mountain/Pier 17 is very well known throughout the Philippines. It is one of those places that if you Google it, you can find plenty of information. It is situated on the coast. Water rushes in and pulls pollution out into the bay, which has become a nasty little inlet. Pollution-wise, it was probably the worst place I have ever seen because of the combination of land and water mixing together in a proverbial garbage stew. Living conditions for the people are very poor. And, there really isn't a whole lot going on ministry-wise that we could see. There was a public school nearby, but we didn't see anyone helping with the kids' nutrition or other programs.

Pastor Reynixon indicated that nutrition was the biggest need in the community. For some time, it had been on his heart to feed the kids and to help with their education so that they could learn and grow and find a way to leave the desperate surroundings in their community. We were intrigued by what we were seeing, but we knew we were going to be visiting four dump communities on that trip, so Jon and I decided not to commit to anything. We told Pastor Reynixon that we were going to see the other three communities and then get back with him to see how we might want to get involved.

After that initial dump visit, Jeff took us back to his mission—Kid's International Ministries. It was the best-run missions housing accommodations we had ever seen. They take care of all your food needs, do all the cooking, and the water is even purified at the facility, which is really rare. They were extremely accommodating, and I took note that if we needed to bring teams to the Philippines, it was very affordable. Our ground costs were half of what they had been in other countries. Jeff even provides local translators and transportation. The table seemed to be set for our ministry, if God led us in that direction.

STAY

On Tuesday, we went to visit the second dump community. It was a very similar scenario. We pulled up to a small church where roughly 250 people were in the courtyard waiting for medical care. The families were not used to having doctors nearby, so they were eager for the opportunity to see one in their community. We got Fran set up with the clinic and met Pastor Joemar Sison, whose church was hosting our medical team. We asked if he could take us down to the dump and tell us more about it. We had driven right past it on our way to the church and wanted to survey the situation. He readily agreed.

Walking into the dump, we didn't see that many people, so we asked if people work on the dump. He told us that we needed to get closer to see the people. We found this statement to be a bit peculiar, but who were we to question him? He then informed us that the dump had been closed for 13 years. But there were still people living around it and working on it. We arrived at the edge of the landfill, and Jon and I looked out over a landscape of crater-like holes. People's heads popped up out of the holes and disappeared. Pastor Joemar told us that they were burrowing all the way down to 20-year-old trash to find old buried metal to recycle.

We walked up to a crater that was probably 10-feet deep, and peeked over the edge to find three guys at the bottom digging away. As we were taking in this new information, Jon asked if we could take pictures. Pastor Joemar told the workers that we were friendly and offering a medical clinic in the community for their families. They graciously granted permission to document their work. As Jon started taking pictures, I was standing on one edge of the giant hole, beginning to zone out. The scene I was witnessing was new for me. I had gotten used to seeing some of the general elements present within dump communities. You see similar things, but this place was different. This landfill had been closed 13 years, but the people were still there. *So is closing a dump really the key to helping the people?* I had asked myself that question many times as the leader of TMP. Logically, we all realize that landfills have to exist and that simply closing one to open another is not necessarily an answer to anything.

I was trying to take in the surreal surroundings of this place, and all of a sudden I unmistakably heard the word "STAY." Startled, every sense in my body jumped to attention when I heard it. I remember looking around to see who was speaking and realized I was alone. Jon was 30 to 40 feet away from me, not paying any attention to what I was doing. I froze ... and I thought *STAY?* I immediately launched into prayer, and I asked God if that was Him speaking, stay where? Stay put, don't move? Or stay here for the day? Or what were we supposed to be doing? I was confused, but it was very clear that the word was STAY. I was amazed by this revelation, but a little more detail would have been great!

Please understand that is not typical for me. I am not someone who is always making a claim that Jesus told me this or that—like I know that God wants me to buy the red car, not the blue one. I was positive it was a message from God. It was nothing else. I had not gone mad, and I was not feeding my own brain through the emotion I was feeling ... that was real. I had not had something like that happen since our crazy experience in Cambodia, and He had definitely gotten my full attention.

A few moments later, Jon walked over. He could tell I was frazzled. I suggested that we take a walk. I quietly told him to pay attention. That something was going on, something was happening. That we needed to be sensitive to whatever God was doing. He agreed to pray, and we continued walking over to the edge of the dump. A bunch of kids had started following us as we walked up a little access road that led to the foot of a ridge that surrounded the landfill, maybe 40 feet high. We looked up and noticed an older gentleman waving and motioning for us to come up and talk with him. We climbed up to the ridge and realized the kids with us belonged to his family.

At the top of the ridge, we saw that there were several little family communities spread along the side of the ridge overlooking the dump. We started talking to the elder of the community and realized that he had some 30 kids and grandchildren living in the small area in which we were standing. The conditions were really heartbreaking and difficult to witness. And as we were talking to him, it clicked. It was so clear that the STAY meant we were supposed to STAY the night with that family. That we were to STAY with the family and, don't ask me how, but my confusion from just minutes earlier had been clarified instantly.

For me, that raised some serious questions. After almost getting killed at the dump in Cambodia, our board had decided that we weren't going to be visiting dump communities at night for any reason. But everything in me said that's exactly what we were supposed to do. Jon and I had always wanted to see what a full day in the life of a recycler was like. And this seemed like the perfect opportunity to do just that.

I leaned over to Jon as Pastor Joemar was talking to the elderly man. I asked what he thought about spending the night out here, one night during that week. He instantly replied, "Yeah, let's do it." And I was thinking, *oh great, thanks...I was kind of hoping for some push back from you. Maybe Fran will think it is a stupid idea and tell me that I am crazy.*

So I turned and told the community elder that we would be honored if we could bring dinner out to his family, bring some tents to spend the night in his community, and work for a day with his kids. We wanted to see what it was like to be a recycler and learn more about what he did...hands on. He gave us a sign of honor that's customary in their culture and said they would be delighted if we would stay with them. He was actually very excited, as no one had ever stayed out in the dump with his family before. Of course, his statement threw up yet another red flag for me, remembering back to Cambodia when they told us that no one had ever filmed in the dump at night.

Then my mind started racing. I thought, *is this a good idea?* I quickly ran through all the logical reasons for why not to do it, even as we were walking away. *What's the board going to say? What's my wife going to say putting her through this, knowing that she nearly lost me the last time I went on a dump at night? Maybe I am misunderstanding God?* I was still convinced that what I heard was for real, but I was struggling with His confirmation of what it meant. The last thing I wanted to do was put Jon and Fran in danger because of my reckless leadership.

CONFIRMATION

Walking back to the church, Jon and I decided we needed to have some time for planning and processing everything we had just experienced. So we made sure Fran had everything under control with the right help for the clinic, because we needed to head back to our room at the house. As we were about to leave, I leaned over and asked Fran, "Hey man, what do you think about spending the night out here sometime this week?" His reply was as quick and positive as Jon's, saying, "Yeah man, let's do it." And I'm thinking, *Wow, OK, everyone else around here has a lot more faith than I do and is not questioning this. Why am I questioning it? Heck, I am the one who just heard an unearthly voice.* I had no push back from the two guys I was inviting. And even Pastor Joemar volunteered to stay the night with us. In just minutes, the whole plan had been put into place. We were going to stay the night in a trash dump community.

So we got in the car and were driving away from the community, and it happened again. I was in the front seat. Jon was in the back with our interpreter, Rick. They were deep in a conversation about cameras, and I had no interest in joining in as I needed to pray about what had just happened. The problem was that my prayer was more about me questioning what it so clearly seemed God was telling me to do. And, at that moment, I was gazing through the window at the dump and as clear as I heard the word STAY, I heard "Matthew 17." I froze. Honestly, I had no idea what "Matthew 17" meant, other than it was an obvious scripture reference.

I slowly pulled out my Bible very intrigued, yet a bit scared to see what it said. As I opened the Gospel of Matthew, I instantly recognized it as the story of the transfiguration. As I read on, the comedic part of that whole chapter was that it uses the word "mountain" three times. I started laughing at that because we were driving down from Trash Mountain.

In the first half of Matthew 17, Jesus was confirming to three of His disciples, Peter, James, and John, who He really was, and showing them His power, because they were continually struggling with their faith in Him. Ironically, there I was having a faith struggle concerning what to do with the command to "stay."

I kept reading the chapter and it moved into the part where Jesus said:

"...O faithless and twisted generation, how long am I to be with you? How long am I to bear with you? Bring him here to me." And Jesus rebuked him, and the demon came out of him, and the boy was healed instantly. Then the disciples came to Jesus privately and said, "Why could we not cast it out?" He said to them, "Because of your little faith. For truly, I say to you, if you have faith like a grain of mustard seed, you will say to this mountain, 'Move from here to there,' and it will move, and nothing will be impossible for you." (Matthew 17:17-20).

Strangely, we were driving away from a mountain at that very moment.

As I was reading, it hit me like a ton of bricks—it was a faith check for me—I felt like I was being called out by God. I started tearing up, and I thought, *my Father has given me a command, and who am I to question Him? We are going to do this. Please forgive me Lord.* God told me to do something, and who was I to say no? I have said that in a spiritual sense, this was one of the greatest and worst moments in my relationship with Jesus Christ.

After having this moment of clarity, I began taking notes about the whole experience. When we are out on the field I am always researching, taking notes of what we see and experience. I turned around and asked Rick for the name of the dump. He said, "San Mateo." And I looked at him, and I asked him if that meant St. Matthew? He replied "Yes." Shivers went up my spine. It was another piece of the puzzle in place. Here I thought I was just driving off of a mountain, hearing from God concerning a command to have the faith to move mountains out of the Book of Saint Matthew. Little did I know that the mountain, itself, was called Saint Matthew. Wow!

We got back to the house, and I told Jon about the Matthew 17 experience. He was stunned. So we decided to spend the night at San Mateo two days later, on Thursday night, after we had visited all four dumps.

After a short night's sleep, still pretty jet lagged, I was up at 4:00 the next morning. I was praying and answering some e-mails (these two things seem to go well together at times) and then Fran appeared in the doorway. I wanted to share with him what was going on since I had asked if he would join us for the night in the dump. I mentioned Matthew 17 to Fran, and he just froze. Then gave me a look like—really? I asked him what was happening. He told me he had a running theme in his life with that chapter, and more in general with Peter, one of Jesus' disciples who was present at the Transfiguration. As a doctor, he would go into places where the people saw and treated him as a healer. He would use medicine, but they called him Peter, as Peter was known as a miraculous healer after Jesus' resurrection and ascension.

Fran went on to share a specific incident years ago with a 12-year-old girl who was dying. She had been in a coma for days, and the family had gathered to spend time with her during her final hours. Medically, there was no hope at that point. The girl was going to eventually pass from the coma into death.

Fran, his wife, Diane, a few family members, and another doctor were praying over the child. As they prayed, the girl opened her eyes, stared directly at Fran and said in clear English, "Who do you think you are, Peter?" Then she immediately went back into the coma. The girl didn't speak a word of English. Everyone in the room turned pale. Fran was concerned that he was hallucinating. But everyone in the room saw it and was freaked out by it, not knowing who or what that was.

I had never heard of anything like what Fran had just shared with me. Dumbfounded, I dug a little deeper and asked him what he thought all this meant. And Fran said that if God spoke Matthew 17 to me, and the chapter so clearly focused on Jesus revealing His true identity to Peter and two others, challenging their lack of faith and relying on God, even after He had revealed Himself...we knew that God was going to do something. All we needed to do was follow Him in faith. Fran was in, and couldn't fully explain how inspiring this was for him. Just another confirmation—what more did I need? We were good to go.

GOOD WORD: SO LITTLE FAITH ~ DR. JIM CONGDON

Matthew 17:17-20 makes the Top 10 list of "most embarrassing moments" for the 12 disciples. They have been with Him for two years now, and Jesus has given them an unusual ability to heal and work miracles. It is not their own ability, of course; he has simply given them access to His power when they pray with faith.

But now they are striking out. There is a demonized boy with epileptic convulsions. The disciples obsess with how bad the boy's condition is, rather than seeing him with eyes of faith in God's omnipotence. And then, rather than turning to prayer, they lean on their own gifts, fail miserably, and then get defensive as the onlookers shake their heads.

It's happened to you, and to me. We were confronted by a BIG problem. Our marriage was on life support. Or our investments evaporated. Or the doctor gave us ghastly news. Or there was a trash dump community that seemed way too poor, too dark, too evil. And our reaction was to get overwhelmed, panic, get defensive, and strike out.

Mark tells us this wasn't an easy healing—the boy had a convulsion that was so bad they thought he was dead. But Jesus' reaction was not to have sympathy for His disciples who faced a big problem. Instead, their lack of faith nearly sent Him over the edge. He's not just disappointed—He's angry, and hurt. *Unbelieving!* He calls them. *Rebellious!* Their faith is so negligible it makes a mustard seed look like a beach ball!

That's embarrassing. And scary. Doesn't it makes you shudder a little, wondering how many times Jesus has felt that way about you? It does me. It's one thing for Jesus to be rejected by His enemies. It's another thing for we, His friends, to let Him down.

Pray this prayer: "Lord, thank You for the reminder that You are a Big God who wants to be asked with a Big Faith for Big Things that will magnify You in Big Ways."

TWO MORE COMMUNITIES

After Fran and I were done talking, we got geared up and went out to the third dump, wondering what was going to happen today. It was a gigantic trash dump called Payatas. We met a woman named Marivic who had worked with the kids in the community for nearly 30 years. Picture a Filipino Mother Teresa, and you've got Marivic. She lives in the dump community with almost nothing. Any money that she gets she uses to buy food, school supplies, and Bibles for the kids who attend her program.

The Payatas landfill has 12 communities of 2,000 people each surrounding it, making it the largest trash dump community in Manila. We met with Marivic and saw her passion and how she interacted with the kids. We were evaluating potential ministry partners and felt like Marivic was our lady. We told her we still had another community to visit the next day, but we wanted to meet with her again before we left the country discuss how we could potentially partner with her ministry.

On Thursday, our fourth day in the Philippines, we visited the final dump community on this trip: Tanza 1, a small district in Antipolo City. As we pulled up, we saw over 300 people waiting for the medical clinic at a huge covered basketball court. Like some of the other sites, we were informed that they had never had a doctor visit to do a clinic within the community. We looked at the massive crowd then looked at Fran and said, "Good luck, buddy!" He had a few volunteers with no medical experience and over 300 people asking for care. So he quickly started seeing patients.

Jon and I talked with the chairman of the community and asked if he could take us up to the landfill. He told us that he could take us back to the dump but that we couldn't go up on it. No one can go on the dump unless they are working there. He told us there were no kids up there at the very moment kids walked by us carrying giant bags of recyclable materials.

Since it was clear that we couldn't enter the dump, we asked if we could go to the perimeter and use a telephoto lens on our camera to take some pictures. He gave us permission to do that, we rode over on "trikes" to the gate, equipped with two security guards. Seeing the guards, we understood what the chairman was saying about not entering the dump.

But as we were standing there and as Jon started taking pictures, I felt what I can only describe as a "nudge" to ask this one specific guard if we could go in. So I turned to the chairman and asked him if he would go ask the guard if we could go through the gates. He said, "No, he couldn't, the man could literally lose his job if he let us enter." I insisted, asking if he could humor me by asking that one specific guard.

I am sure he was irritated with the request, (with the "dumb American" look on his face), but he went over to talk with the guy. The guard instantly got a glazed look on his face, said yes, and opened the gate. The chairman turned around, looked at me and shook his head. He told us to move quickly because that never happened, and we didn't want the guard to change his mind. So we hopped back on the trikes. As we cruised past the guards, Jon held his camera up and gestured, pictures? Can I take pictures? And the guard said, "Sure."

Driving up the huge side of a mountain, I leaned back and asked Jon if he noticed that the guard seemed like he didn't have control over what he was saying. Jon laughed, having noticed the same thing. So we both started joking that it was like a Jedi mind trick! But we brushed it off, thinking maybe that's just how the guy was. We didn't want to argue with him as he was being very hospitable to us.

We went up to the top of the dump and shot some video footage, met some of the people, and saw the working and living conditions—some of the workers were living on the dump itself. But, within about 15 minutes, we had worn out our welcome. They were not used to having Americans with cameras in their place of work, and understood that we were their guests. I suggested that we leave, not wanting to impose ourselves, especially since the guard had been so kind to us already.

We drove back down the side of the mountain to the gate. The guard opened the gate, waved, smiled, and said, "Thank you!" Strangely, he had that same glazed look on his face that he had when we entered. We got back to the medical clinic, and the chairman began talking with one of the community pastors, who looked over at us and said that that doesn't happen! He didn't know why the guard let us in the dump.

As we were leaving the dump, right outside the entrance, I had noticed what appeared to be a church off to the right. Upon our return to the medical clinic, I asked the chairman and a local pastor about any churches in the area. He told us there was a small Baptist church, a Catholic church, a charismatic church, and a

Wesleyan church—the one I had noticed outside the entrance to the dump. Having attended Asbury Theological Seminary and growing up in the Wesleyan church, I was really encouraged. I have always looked for a possible partnership with a Wesleyan church. I have a great deal of respect for the denomination, so I asked if we could go back and check it out.

In my mind, I was thinking of taking some pictures of the building, getting the name of the church and any other information on it and then reporting back to my former pastor back home, Ed Rotz, District Superintendent of the Kansas Wesleyan Church. I wanted to check with him to see if he knew anything about the Vista Wesleyan Church in the Tanza 1 community. Did he know who the pastor was, what they did, and if they had any special needs? I figured that if anyone could help us with our questions, he could. We finished up the clinic and had to race away to get out to San Mateo before dark so that we could set up camp in the community for our night's stay. Nothing could have prepared us for the journey we were about to begin.

Chapter 14:

RETURNING TO DARKNESS

———•———

W e arrived back at the mission house, and our host had everything set for us: dinner for the family and tents for us to stay in out at San Mateo. And then we had another comedic, light moment. We figured he'd give us one tent and we'd all stay in it, but he gave us three tents. Remember the transfiguration story, (the Matthew 17 moment from a few days before) with the three tents that Peter offered to build for Jesus, Elijah, and Moses. We were joking about it—trying to keep it light, because we were all nervous—wondering who was bold enough to be Jesus?

Arriving at San Mateo, we met up with Pastor Joemar, who had graciously offered to stay the night with us for safety. He had a young man with him named Don Don, a former street kid and gang member who the church had rescued years ago. We walked over to the community where we had met the elder just a few days earlier. His entire family was there, and they were all excited by our visit to their home. We enjoyed getting to know the family over a dinner of prawns and rice, which was their requested dish.

As we were setting up our tents preparing for the night, a termite storm hit the community. In something resembling a biblical plague, tens of thousands of termites flew in like a cloud.

We had no idea that something like this even existed. We had our shirts up over our faces and couldn't really breathe or talk or we would end up with them in our mouths. The people started burning some trash in an effort to repel the termites. We huddled around the trash fire, and we all thought we were going to be ill breathing in some 15-year-old garbage. Not knowing what else to do, after a long period of standing in front of the fire, we decided to get in our tents.

Before we got into our tents, the family told us that they go out and work in the dump in shifts: one shift at midnight and a second at 5:00 AM, because it is a lot cooler at night in the heat of the summer. We decided to join the 5:00 AM crew so we could at least get some sleep. Once we got set up, we were glad to have our two friends with us—the more the merrier—and it made us feel more secure in our unknown surroundings. They sat up right outside our tents and said that we could go to bed while they kept watch.

Fran fell asleep and was snoring in less than five minutes. We couldn't believe it, as there wasn't a chance on earth that we were going to fall asleep within the hour, and certainly not in five minutes. Jon and I were sweating bullets, uncomfortable as can be and were hearing the constant motion of people outside the tents. We wondered what was happening. For this community, seeing two Americans and a Filipino camped out with cameras and video gear could be too much of a temptation for theft or worse.

I sent texts to my wife throughout the night (go AT&T) to let her know we were okay, as I knew she was very nervous about us being there. Upon my return home, she told me with tears in her eyes that she thought that when I spoke to her on our drive out to San Mateo it would be the last time she ever heard my voice. The whole time I was there, thoughts of me dying flooded her mind. How would she explain that to our four children? Would they all hate God because I died following what I interpreted as a command from Him? How would she raise our kids alone? Let's just say that my beautiful bride has been through a lot, and that I honestly believe that she is the strongest wife and mother on the face of the planet.

Throughout the night, I peeked out of the tent every half hour or so as I kept hearing Don Don and Pastor Joemar talking to each other. They seemed to have conversations with all the people wandering by and kept things light about the strange houseguests in the tents as they offered them fresh water on their way to work at the dump. At one point, it started raining, and I figured they had gone for cover because they were not there when I looked out. Then I finally fell asleep for a couple of hours during the rain.

When I awoke at 4:30 AM, I looked outside before exiting the tent, and there they were still sitting at the corners of our tents. I looked over at them, and I asked if they had slept. They said, "No." I told them they should have gotten in our tents or we could have set up something for them. And they said, "No, they were there to watch out for us." I pressed further, still arguing with them. Finally Don Don stopped me and he said, "No, you don't understand. We are here to protect you. God told us to protect you, as you are our guests." The way he said it was just as nonchalant as if he was telling me he enjoyed dinner last night. It was just a fact.

That was a very sobering moment. These guys barely knew us. I don't think they had any idea how much their actions meant to us. Or how much they were doing to teach us about what it really looks like to be in Christian community and care for one another; to love each other; to BE the church for one another. They had literally embraced the biblical role of a watchman. I am sure it was more difficult for me to process this in light of my experiences in Cambodia. From what we could tell, God had sent guardians once again to look out for us, only this time they did show up in pictures and were most definitely human. God always protected and guided us throughout this journey. I just wonder who was praying at the moment God sent our two guardians that night.

A DAY IN THE LIFE

Rising after a short, restless night, we gathered our equipment and went down to the dump with some of the children from the community. Little did we know that we were about to have one of the most sobering moments of our lives. As the three of us positioned ourselves in a shallow hole on the dump, we were taught by three-, four- and five-year-olds how to pick through the trash to make enough money to eat the next day. We worked for about two-and-a-half hours and were completely exhausted—and only made about 25 cents among the three of us. Of course, we didn't know what we were doing, but we are also able-bodied grown men. We wondered how anyone could support a family doing this. After failing miserably at our work duty, we walked around the dump and noticed that the majority of the workers were kids. We later learned that over 80 % of the children in that community were not attending school.

After our time with the five AM work crew, we returned to our host family for an interview with the community elder. We wanted to hear his story. How did he and his family end up there? As Jon and I began the interview, Don Don walked up to me and handed me a blue Nike shirt. I asked him what it was. He told me that I was really sweaty and dirty and covered in trash, and he wanted me to take his shirt. I responded, "Dude, I can't take your shirt." I was thinking that he probably owned only three shirts, and I couldn't take one of them. I said, "It's OK, I'm dirty—I'll just stay dirty." His face sank, and he replied it would be an honor for him if I took his shirt. His facial expression said it all. It meant a great deal to him for me to take his shirt. It was a gesture of respect and love. So I accepted the shirt, turned around to go put it on, had an emotional moment, and came back to attempt to process all that was going on around me.

On a later returning trip to the Philippines, we visited with Don Don and talked about that night. When we asked him why he stayed out there with us, he replied, "I was willing to give my life to protect the three of you because I knew that God had sent you. I would have done whatever it took as that was what God had commanded of me." I hope that this resonates with anyone reading it the way that it did with us. That man, who didn't previously know us at all was willing to give his life for us; more accurately, for God. He is a living, breathing embodiment of the Gospel message "to go therefore and make disciples of all nations...and that greater love has no one than this, that someone lay down his life for his friends" (Matthew 28:19a; John 15:13, ESV).

After my interaction with Don Don, we began our interview with the elder. He said that none of them wanted this life, but it was the only livelihood they had. And when we asked him what he had faith in, he replied that it was simple: he had faith in the dump as it provided for their daily needs and was their only means of survival. We asked if he had faith in anything other than the dump. He said, no, because there was nothing else to care for them, and there was nothing else that could give them food. Since that time, he and his family have become a part of

Pastor Joemar's church. They have seen that there is more to their life than what they have found in the garbage dump. There is, in fact, a God that cares for them and wants them to thrive here on earth and in the life to come.

The elder continued to tell us their story and explain what their reality was like. He told us that he knew it must seem cruel that they send their young children out to work the dump, but the reality is that if they don't work today, they don't eat tomorrow.

Not once at any time during that interview or during the duration of our visit to this community did anyone ask us for anything. To me, that was impressive. Throughout that overwhelming experience and seeing how high the need was, not a single person asked for money or other assistance. They didn't see us as an opportunity for a handout. They just welcomed us as their guests.

After finishing the interview and packing up our gear, we went up on top of the mountain directly behind the community. We prayed for everyone we had met during our stay. We were emotionally and spiritually spent at that point, so we thanked our two watchmen and headed back down one last time to say goodbye to our new friends in the community.

EUGENE

Upon saying our goodbyes, we noticed a little boy who had been sitting on his mother's lap the whole time we were there. Before we left the dump to return to the mission center, the three of us walked up to their small bamboo home. As we approached, the boy began screaming and crying. Jon and I backed off while Fran told the mother that he was a physician and asked if he could help. It was apparent that the boy could not walk, and Fran wanted to examine his medical condition. Finally the boy calmed down, and Fran was able to talk to her and look at his legs.

The boy's name was Eugene. He was eight-years-old and had undergone a surgery due to an infection in his legs when he was 11-months-old. Ever since, he had not been able to stand or walk. After examining him, Fran said there was nothing he could do as the damage to his muscles and other tissue was too extensive. He explained that in his condition there was no surgery that could be provided to help him either. He would remain lame for the rest of his life.

The three of us felt compelled to pray, as we fully believed that God would heal his legs and that he would stand and walk. After all, He had brought us all together through a little girl that He rescued from death's door. If God could revive and heal a young girl dying of AIDS, He could surely heal the legs of this boy. We prayed with his mother for his healing, and all of us honestly thought that as we opened our eyes Eugene would be standing there...but nothing happened. We all expected him to stand up and walk, but he didn't. It was a down note to leave on, but we knew it was in God's hands.

As we were driving away, I looked over at Jon and Fran. I started to question why, with all the craziness leading up to staying the night out there, were we supposed to do it. Were we going to see some wild miracle, like someone's arm grow back, or something that we've never seen before? But, at that moment, we realized that that wasn't the point. The point was that God was teaching us why we do what we do—it is for the people. The message was very clear. This is why Trash Mountain Project exists.

Then to see the demonstration of love and true discipleship in the two guys who watched over us—we couldn't have learned more in one day. One was a recovered street kid and gang member who had nothing. And the other was an unpaid pastor who had very little in this world. They only had a heart for Christ, and that was all they needed. That was why we had come, and why God had told us to "stay." His purpose was to teach and inspire us. No one's arm grew back, and no one got killed, but little did we know that the story had not ended with our prayer for Eugene—something supernatural did, in fact, happen!

Chapter 15:

WASTE PLACES

———◆———

"Listen to me, you who pursue righteousness, you who seek the Lord: look to the rock from which you were hewn, and to the quarry from which you were dug. Look to Abraham your father and to Sarah who bore you; for he was but one when I called him, that I might bless him and multiply him. For the Lord comforts Zion; he comforts all her WASTE PLACES." (Isaiah 51:1-3a)

Being just a bit overwhelmed by our experience, we took a day to process all that had happened during our stay at San Mateo. After some downtime, we turned our attention to the other communities we had visited. I had already e-mailed Ed Rotz back in Topeka about the Wesleyan church we had discovered in Tanza 1. I received an e-mail back from him that the General Superintendent of the Philippine Wesleyan Church was a man named Dr. Alberto Patacsil. He explained that it would be customary for me to send Dr. Patacsil an e-mail to explain what our intentions were in meeting with the pastor of one of the churches under his leadership umbrella. But Ed didn't think he lived in the area where we were staying in Manila, and it would be unlikely for us to actually meet him in person, as he was a very busy man. So there was no reason to try and meet with him; just make contact with him in some fashion. Ed was going to gather the information we needed and send it my way. But he also recommended that we could go to the church on Sunday and attend services with their congregation. I agreed.

On Sunday morning, we traveled to Vista Wesleyan Church and met Pastor Stanley Rabago. He asked what we were visiting for and what we do, and we told him we worked for a ministry called Trash Mountain Project. We told him we work in trash dump communities, internationally partnering with local churches and ministries to share the Gospel, but didn't really get into any of the details as it is important for us to hear the vision of local leaders that we encounter so as to not change or influence what God is already doing within the communities we visit. And, with that in mind, I asked him about his church and their vision for the community. As he began to speak, he could have been reading our mission statement from our web site. He explained their passion to develop programs in education, discipleship, self-sustainability, livelihood projects, clean water, nutrition, healthcare, and technical training. Jon and I were on cloud nine hearing the passion in this man's voice—it was our shared passion! What his church wanted was a perfect fit for partnership with our ministry, because we wanted to partner with vision, not force our vision on anyone else.

As we shared our similar vision, he became visibly excited. In conversation, we went on to tell him about going up on the dump a few days earlier when we were hosting the medical clinic. About mid-sentence he stopped me and, with a perplexed look on his face, said, "What? You went up on the dump?" We nodded and said, "Yes." He then questioned, "How did you do that? Did you get some kind of permit or something?" He looked totally confused. I said, "No, we just asked the guard." We told Stanley jokingly that the guy didn't seem to know what he was telling us to do. And we all had a good laugh as we repeated the Jedi mind trick theory. As we were laughing, he said, "I have been a pastor here for seven years, and I've never been up there. They've never let me go up there." With a serious look on his face, he said, "That was God! There's no other way to explain it. That was God, and if you don't recognize it let me tell you again, that was God!"

We knew it was unusual, but I don't think we quite grasped the gravity of what had happened that day. Realizing it was almost time for church to start, we told him we knew he needed to go begin worship, but that we were going to be sticking around and hoped to talk more after service. And then right before he turned around, I asked if he knew Dr. Alberto Patacsil? He started smiling and replied that Dr. Patacsil was his general superintendent. He then went on to ask if we wanted to meet with him. With an enthusiastic yes, we asked how that would be possible. He informed us that he just happened to be speaking that afternoon at the dedication ceremony of a new inner-city ministry property in Manila. We had planned to go see some waterfall that day for fun after church, but this was a no-brainer. What an opportunity!

ISAIAH 51

Returning to the mission center after church, we informed Jeff that there was a change of plans. Instead of the trip to the waterfall, we now needed a ride to a certain spot at a certain time at a certain address in the city. He made the arrangements, and communicated the plan to our driver. We loaded up in the vehicle and were excited, thinking that this could be something big.

We'd been driving about an hour, and it seemed like we were going out of town, but who were we to question our driver. From what I understood, the event at the Wesleyan church was right in the center of the city. And I was looking around and wondering if we went the wrong way. Then I saw a sign for the waterfall. The driver must have had it in his head that we were going to the waterfall, even though he was told otherwise. He didn't speak any English, but somehow I stopped him and I said

Church—Iglesia—Wesleyan. I was trying to explain and he got a serious look on his face like he knew he had made a mistake.

I called Jeff and told him what was going on and put our driver on the phone. After a minute or so the driver gave me back the phone, and Jeff informed me we were a long way from our destination—the opposite direction, in fact. We were two-and-a-half hours away from the event that was scheduled to end in an hour-and-a-half. We explained how important reaching our destination was to us, and put him back on the phone with our driver. A few moments later, he hung up, wheeled the car around, looked at us with a serious look on his face and in broken English said, "I will get you there." And we were off, OH MY!

The next thing you know, we were flying around mountain curves at breakneck speeds. Jon and I began discussing that this may, in fact, be how we go down, and we should probably say a quick prayer for safety and that God would get us to our meeting. I was in the front seat struggling to keep my lunch down, and was also processing through the overwhelming reality I'd seen over the previous week of how bad the dump community problem was surrounding this beautiful city. I started to worry. I was coping with the anxiety over that place and what we were going to do and how we were going to do it. I was also worried that we would miss the chance to meet a key leader in the Filipino Church because our driver had taken us the wrong direction. Then it happened. In the midst of my pity party, for the third time in six days, I heard that now familiar voice..."Isaiah 51." I turned to Jon and told him I would throw up if I tried to look down and read something and asked him to read the passage I had just heard. Jon, trooper that he is, said sure, but if I puke you know where it is going to land.

I had no clue what was in that seemingly random passage of Scripture. I had studied Isaiah in seminary, but I'm no Old Testament scholar. As Jon started to read, it was one of the most astonishing things I had ever heard. He got three verses in and it says, "He comforts all her waste places." He paused as tears filled our eyes. It was funny, because as incredible as this was, I became disappointed in myself, because as the leader of a ministry that serves in waste places, I was not aware of this verse in Scripture.

As Jon continued reading, we realized that the whole chapter is about redemption and about God rebuilding the physical waste places and about rebuilding the downtrodden, the people who had been broken, bringing restoration, hope, and salvation to a broken community. It was a staggering moment. The Lord was basically saying, "Shut up and stop worrying, I've got you, you're worried about this, this is just traffic, I've got this." I was instantly at total peace with the situation. If we were supposed to get there, we would get there. And, amazingly, it was like the Red Sea of traffic had parted and the driver somehow got us to our destination through the gigantic, traffic-filled metropolis of Manila.

We pulled up to our destination, walked in, and within minutes after arriving Dr. Patacsil finished speaking and walked off the stage. But he walked straight through the large crowd looking directly at us. He grabbed two chairs, and asked us to please sit down and tell him about Trash Mountain Project. He had a very serious look on his face, so we quickly gave him the five-minute elevator speech about our ministry.

After describing our mission, Dr. Patacsil started looking down at the ground, and then locked eyes with me and said, "The minute you started speaking, my heart filled with joy. We have been trying to reach that community for so long, and we are at a loss. We are really struggling with what to do to have a long-term impact in the Tanza 1 community."

He was about to say something else, but he held back. He was NOT saying something. I wondered what that was, but it really didn't matter. He went on to tell us we were there for a reason. He asked what we were doing the next day. We said it was our last day in the Philippines and had planned to climb a volcano and hit golf balls into it—which must have sounded pretty stupid. "But," I said, "What's up? You tell us, what are we doing tomorrow?"

He told us to return to that location at 10:00 AM for a meeting he was having with every district superintendent for the entire country for the Wesleyan Church. He was scheduled to speak to them for 30 minutes about reaching the lost and the forgotten people of their country. He said he would love to give me 20 of his 30 minutes! Would I speak to their leaders? And I thought, *Whoa, what just happened here? We went from meeting the pastor of the church in the community to meeting the church superintendent of the entire country and then being invited to speak to every superintendent of every district. Of course!* We told him that he could count on us to be there the next morning.

We got in the car to return back to the mission center. We were laughing, we were crying—what just happened? On our return, we told our host of the change of plans, again. We needed to be at that same location at 10 AM the next day; please make sure the driver knows the correct location.

I quickly e-mailed Pastor Ed to tell him what was going on and received an almost instant e-mail back stating that he was overwhelmed. He had never heard of anything like what we were experiencing. He encouraged us to go with it, that whatever was happening was God—don't question it.

GOOD WORD: WASTE PLACES ~ DR. JIM CONGDON

You are reading one of the most inspiring chapters in this book. If your heart doesn't swell with pleasure at the glory and wisdom of God in this chapter, there's something wrong with you!

The Hebrew word translated "waste place" (*ghor-bah*) is used about 40 times in the Old Testament and refers to a desolate, desert place. Often it is a place that God has judged and destroyed.

Here in Isaiah 51:3, it describes the condition of God's nation Israel after enemies have overrun and destroyed it. God is promising that He will restore and rebuild it, fill it with joy and make it beautiful like the Garden of Eden. God says that when the waste places are "rebuilt," then "you will know that I am the Lord" (Ezekiel 36:11, ESV).

I think this can be taken as a promise that if you are one of God's people, and your life has become a "waste place," that God has not turned away from you forever, but intends to restore you, rebuild you, and turn you into a Garden of Eden!

But this gives a wonderful insight into the ultimate purpose of TMP. Admittedly, the trash landfills around the world are not "Christian" places where God's judgment has fallen on His chosen people—so God is not promising that He will turn each and every one of the world's trash mountains into a Garden of Eden!

But here's the point: when TMP goes to a trash mountain, and brings the Lord to it, and builds homes and schools and churches, it brings the blessing of God to bear on a "waste place," thereby applying the Isaiah 51/Ezekiel 36 blessing to it:

It is bringing the greatest knowledge of all, the knowledge "that I am the Lord."

It is bringing the joy of the Lord to a place without joy and hope.

It is turning part of a trash dump community into a Garden of Eden.

FILLED WITH JOY

We left for the meeting the next morning and, with a smile, our driver mentioned that we would go straight there with no detour. Upon our arrival, Dr. Patacsil got up to address that crowd of leaders and said, "We have some guests from the United States. But before I introduce them, I need to say something. A lot of you know the struggle that we have had out at our church in the Tanza 1 dump community—Pastor Stanley's church—and trying to figure out how to reach that segment of our society. It's a sub-culture that we don't really understand. Then yesterday, these two gentlemen walked into our lives, and they happen to specialize in reaching out to trash dump communities. We have been praying for this…"

He stopped again, like the day before, and hesitated, and *didn't* say something, and I caught it again. "But since meeting them yesterday, I've been praying, and I know for a fact that this is of God. We are committed to partnering with you," Dr. Patacsil continued while looking directly at me and Jon. "You now have over 400 Wesleyan churches throughout the country as your ministry partners—you just tell us what you need from us, and we are there."

The crowd clapped, and I was thinking, *this was before I even said a word. The leader of this church just said what?* I smiled and said thank you. And I got up and showed them the video Jon had created the night before, which gave them a much better picture of what many of them had probably never seen within their country. Pastor Stanley was in tears. I don't remember all I said. But I did talk about how to reach the lost and forgotten people within their trash dump communities. I explained that we by no stretch had all the answers, but that we were committed to serving alongside of them in this mission.

When I finished, everyone stood up and shook our hands. A few of the superintendents told us where they were from and about the dump communities located in their districts. Most said they had wanted to help but didn't know what to do, and they asked us to come and visit. And I was taken right back to feeling overwhelmed. The four dumps just multiplied to how many? From the dump communities we knew, we had now estimated at least 18 throughout the country. Later we discovered that we were way off in our estimate.

Right before we got in the car to leave, Dr. Patacsil grabbed me and asked if I knew Kentucky. I replied that if he meant the state, I used to live there while attending Asbury. He went on to explain that the global Wesleyan Church General Conference, held every fourth year, was in Lexington, Kentucky in two weeks. He would be attending and wondered if Pastor Ed Rotz would be there as he would love to meet him. I said I was sure he would be attending, especially since it was being held just a 10-hour drive from his hometown of Topeka. I informed him that I would talk with Ed and get back to him with a tentative plan for the two of them to meet while attending the conference.

Driving away from our meeting with the Wesleyan Church leaders, it was really hard for Jon and I to get our heads around what we had just experienced. At the start of our first trip to the Philippines, we had very few expectations other than that we knew God had directed our path, and that any time He does that, be ready to follow His move and leading. So many times, it is difficult for us to have clarity concerning His direction, as it is not as simple as calling Him on the phone or getting a planning document from heaven telling us what to do. But, there are those unique times, times that He makes it so blatantly obvious what we are to do, that we would simply have to disobey His command to not follow. This was one of those times.

WHY TMP?

After saying our goodbyes to everyone we had met throughout the trip, we began our long journey home to the United States. Upon our return, we were trying to figure out what in the world had just happened on our first journey to the Philippines. I quickly met up with Pastor Ed and his wife, Sharon, to share the whole story of what had transpired. They were rendered speechless and said they didn't know how to respond. As I was talking with them, I told them that I needed their guidance on something. They had always been a spiritual guide in my life, and I needed their help in processing all of the things that had happened surrounding the Trash Mountain ministry. The whole concept of hearing a voice with no human origin, and then having that voice confirmed by events that followed, what was that? With a smile on her face, Sharon quickly responded, "Brett, look at the people this ministry serves. You and everyone else who is a part of TMP are serving the poorest people on the planet. Why do you think these things are happening? Because God has commanded you—He has commanded us all to do this."

I pressed further because it is not like we are the only ones serving poor communities throughout the world, and I know plenty of people who are doing just that, who have never experienced this kind of thing. Ed responded, "Brett, many times God does things that we can't explain. This is one of those times. You just need to respond by thanking Him and following His lead as He leads you." He was right. It was not important why these things were happening, and it wasn't even important why they were happening to me. What was important is that He was invading the earthly realm to reach out to the desperate children He loves so deeply. It was enough for me.

As we were finishing up our lunch, I asked them if they were going to the General Conference in Kentucky and had time to meet Dr. Patacsil. They were, in fact, going and asked if Jon and I would like to come. We all felt that it was important to be there for that meeting as well. The Wesleyan Church offered to cover our expenses. Jon and I went to Kentucky, and the final act of this story unfolded in dramatic fashion.

We met up with Dr. Patacsil a few times at the conference. Over lunch with he and his wife, Dorcas, and Ed, he and Ed started talking. They went into leader mode and Ed said, "You can trust this guy. I just want you to know that you can trust him," referring to me. And Dr. Patascsil said that his recommendation and trust meant a lot. And he told Ed that he could trust Pastor Stanley. "I didn't tell you this but he is my godson. So we have a real heart for him and that community."

And then the thing I think he was holding back the previous times we had met in the Philippines started coming out. He began tearing up and looked at his wife, and she started tearing up, and we were all thinking, *Oh man, what's he about to say? I had been waiting for this from the time I sensed he was holding back.* And he said they had been praying together every night for the past year for God to send somebody to help with that community and partner with Stanley and his wife, Noreen, at Vista Wesleyan Church. "There is no doubt in my mind, it is you! That's all I know. We know God has ordained this partnership and that TMP was sent to fill that role," he finished.

As those words came out, it clicked. I told him that the funny thing was that we were praying the opposite of his prayer, from here in the States, asking God to give us an opportunity to be used as an answer to someone else's prayer. As they were praying their prayer, we were praying that if someone else is out there praying that prayer—send us—get us there and we'll do what we can to follow.

By the end of that lunch meeting, it was confirmed that hundreds of Filipino leaders were ready and waiting to partner with TMP. This fact was more than a big deal. The hardest thing to do in an international ministry location is to build relationships and have trusted partners on the field. It's beyond unusual to have it happen instantly like that, and to have Jeff Long and his ministry in place with the housing and all the people there who are passionate about what God is doing through TMP. Even Rick, who was originally the man who researched the dump communities around Manila and translated for us has become instrumental in the founding of TMP Philippines as he ran with the vision after our departure.

CONNECTING THE DOTS

Now, go back to the beginning of this whole crazy story; the Cambodia experience and the guy who was our translator.

He was the man who talked to the truck driver and passengers who warned us to get the heck out of there. And he was the first to tell me about the Philippines trash dump problem. He had mentioned a large dump that had to be closed, and it hit me; he was talking about San Mateo. I looked it up and realized that the trash dumps he had mentioned in a communication with me were the very same ones we visited on our trip. The only one he hadn't mentioned, Tanza 1, hadn't been built yet—and part of the reason it was opened was to handle the garbage that would have been going to San Mateo prior to its closure.

The most recent time I had heard from God in a very clear, audible fashion, in a manner different than ordinary prayer, was in the trash dump in the Philippines that the pastor from Cambodia told me about. The time before that was two years earlier in Cambodia, just one day after the pastor had told me about the very dump where I would hear the word "Stay" and "Matthew 17." It was as if there was a huge arrow pointing towards the Philippines the whole time, and I just hadn't seen it. While we were in Cambodia, God's timing was for us to go to the Philippines a couple of years later. And we "happened" to choose a week when all the activity was happening with the Wesleyan Church.

On top of this, the main event that led us to take our first trip to the Philippines was meeting a doctor we only met because God healed a child of an incurable disease. The timing was so staggering and so connected that we made an instant decision to move forward with the Philippines as our next ministry location. We knew we were to move forward, we just didn't know, yet, how God would provide the resources for that step of faith.

Chapter 16:

THE FRUIT OF FAITH

———•◦•———

I t is hard for me to not mention everyone and every crazy event that has been a part of the Trash Mountain story. But for the sake of space and time, I can only report on specific events that lead to each major move of God. I believe He is behind every single person and move that happens within this ministry, but there was a specific response from the people in Topeka, Kansas, on October 14, 2012, that had a significant impact on the future of our ministry, as well as the remaining part of this story.

In 2011, we made the decision to hold our very first large-scale benefit event for the ministry. We called it Spoken. It was held at Fellowship Bible Church in Topeka in the fall of that year. Due to the overwhelming success of the benefit, we decided to make it an annual event. We knew from the fact that we sold out in 2011, and the rapid growth in church partnerships, donors, and volunteers, that it would be a much larger-scale event in 2012.

In Topeka there are only a handful of venues that we can host an event the size of what we were planning. None of them allow you to have your own chef— a deal-breaker for us as having Chefs Robert and Molly Krause to prepare our dinner was non-negotiable. The first venue that came to mind was where Jaelle and I had our wedding reception: the Sunflower Ballroom at the Capital Plaza Hotel.

I knew from our wedding experience and the fact that it has the reputation of being the nicest event venue in town that it would not be the most economical place to host an event. But, I decided to check into it anyway. My cousin Jon works in hotel management, does catering and event coordination, and had helped us with the first Spoken event. I called to see if he had any connections with Capital Plaza as he had worked there as a banquet manager in the past. He knew the Director of Catering, Rob Bergquist, and suggested I mention his name if I called the hotel. I told him what I was thinking, and he said it never hurts to ask, but just know that it would likely be really expensive, and it was against hotel policy to bring in an outside chef.

Rob agreed over the phone to a face-to-face meeting, but from the tone of his voice, I figured he was just humoring me. When I finally met Rob and his boss, I began by explaining the mission of Trash Mountain Project. They mentioned they had looked on our website and knew a little bit about our mission. I explained the details of our first Spoken event that had sold out 300 seats and that this year we needed a much larger facility. I next talked about Robert Krause and how instrumental he had been in setting up our nutrition program in the Dominican Republic and also catering at the first Spoken event. We really wanted him to be the chef for the evening, as he would do it at a top level and at no cost to the ministry.

They were familiar with Robert. And I was relieved to have that issue on the table as I knew it was a long shot. They asked what else we needed for the evening to be a success, and I made a few suggestions. Rob was taking notes the whole time I was talking, and he soon asked when we planned to do the event. He seemed pleased that it would be on a Sunday as that was typically a slow day for them. After sharing all of our needs for the event, they said that they would love to partner with us and unexpectedly approved Robert to be our chef for the event. I shook their hands and walked away wondering what had just happened. It seemed that the biggest mountain blocking the event had just moved. But I still had a bit of a concern for the cost, even though they said they would work on the price for us.

Robert Krause and Gayla Greening attended the second meeting with me to work out the details and be sure that the offer was for real. As we were sitting there, Rob slid me the contract for the event. As I turned to the final page, I couldn't believe the price I saw at the bottom and quickly realized it must have been the deposit. But, when I inquired about the total cost estimate for the event, he informed me that the amount on the final page was the entire cost and that we could not only bring our own food, but we could store it on site! They were even going to write a letter to their food supplier to seek a donation of food as well. I was speechless.

Just to be clear, Robert asked if they were OK with him doing the prep and cooking in their main kitchen. They were not only good with that, but their master chef, Andy, offered to be Robert's sous chef at no additional cost. Andy was ready to volunteer his time for the event because he thought we were working for a great cause, and he wanted to be a part of it. He even allowed Robert and his team to be in the main kitchen the entire week leading up to the event to prep all the food. Robert kept shooting me a look that said *this doesn't happen.*

We took a walk through the facilities, and I asked if they had linens, silverware, and dishes, that we could rent through them so that we didn't have to go to a rental company and haul them over for the event. Rob looked at me and smiled as he explained that all of those items were included in the cost they had quoted us. We were given everything we would need for the event at no additional cost. He basically said, if they had it, we could use it. Additionally, they even approved that we could bring in our own technical director—Wyatt Johnston, who is the Technical Arts Director at Fellowship Bible Church.

I was still thinking there had to be a catch somewhere in the fine print. There was no catch. As we were walking away, I showed the $1,000 price tag to Robert and detailed everything that they were going to provide for the event. He stopped, turned and looked at me, and said, "Brett, this just doesn't happen. I have been in this business for a really long time, and I have never seen anything like this. How do you know them again?" I replied, "I don't."

TWO BOYS DIE

Anyone can attest to the fact that witnessing the devastation of third-world poverty leaves a deep impression in your soul. There is no getting used to it. If I ever become numb to it, I should just go ahead and quit my job and move on to something else. I am far from numb to it. I have struggled deeply with PTSD-like (post-traumatic stress disorder) symptoms during and after many of my trips to trash dump communities. Sometimes having flashbacks to things I have seen or heard, becoming depressed and overwhelmed by the need, or simply breaking down in tears as I pray for those we are called to serve. Many times, it is the smallest thing, such as seeing a picture of devastation that sends me spiraling downward into a deep sadness.

I wish I were stronger and that I could handle what I have been called to do without becoming emotionally attached, but I can't. I honestly believe that one of the reasons God has given us our emotions is so that we can respond with compassion, love, and justice to those in need. Our entire team has dealt with this kind of thing in one form or another. So, I guess it is normal.

I believe it is also normal for us to get back to the grind of being in the office, in meetings, replying to e-mails, and phone calls, and almost block out what it is that we are actually doing within this ministry. We are serving God and His hurting children. Unfortunately, sometimes it takes something horrible happening to remind us of the reality that the people living in trash dump communities face on a daily basis.

On August 10, 2012, I received such a reality check via a Facebook message from Rick Aranas, our friend in the Philippines. I recall the day I received his message as we were working through all of the planning for the Spoken event. We had become very excited about the early response we had received from ticket sales, and were on cloud nine. But then I pulled up my Facebook account, and everything changed in an instant. As I began reading Rick's message, my heart sank. He was informing us that two of the children from the community we stayed at in San Mateo had just passed away from malnutrition. Not only this, but we had met the children.

He asked if I could remember the main boy and his younger brother that were teaching us how to pick through the trash the morning we worked at the dump. I did remember them, and strangely Jon had a really incredible picture of them that we both put as desktop backgrounds on our computers. We were even joking about the fact that we had both put the picture up randomly on the same day. Sadly, the two youngest boys had died from malnutrition. Our hearts broke.

I felt such a deep pain in my chest as I read his words. But that pain quickly turned to an intense anger. I thought: *Why those kids? Why was it the very ones who were so kind to us even though we were outsiders just trying to understand what their lives were like? We slept just feet away from these boys and were only concerned with our own safety. How selfish! We prayed for the boy who couldn't walk, and nothing happened. We wanted to help with providing food for these kids, the very thing that could have saved the two boys, but our ministry didn't have enough money to do so at the time. But do I care? I make a good living and only deal with first-world problems...why couldn't I have done something? Where was I in their moment of need?*

After going to the gym and blowing off some steam, I met with Jon to talk about what we had just learned. We both felt responsible. Even though we didn't know they were in such serious trouble, maybe we could have worked harder and moved faster or raised more money to feed them. Many people have said to me that that kind of thing just happens, and that I shouldn't feel responsible because we are doing so many other great things for those in need around the world. I disagree! If God shows us a need, it has just become our responsibility. I fully understand that we can't help everyone, but we can sure love everyone, and I felt as though I hadn't truly loved these two boys.

I know that our young brothers are in God's hands now, and that they are in a much better place, but I can tell you that this only motivated us to work harder than ever to move the Trash Mountain Project ministry forward. We all knew that for us to help the multitude of children facing the same fate, we needed to gather resources, and we had a huge event just around the corner to do just that. We continued to pray that something as simple as an event would become a game changer.

ANSWERED PRAYERS

As the Spoken event drew near, I began to struggle with how nice the Sunflower Ballroom was. Even though we were paying pennies on the dollar to use it, I didn't want it to appear that we had dropped a lot of money on the event. Additionally, even though we probably had unrestricted funds to pay for the event in full, we prayed that God would provide an underwriter to cover the entire cost so that all of our current funding and funds that we would raise that night would go entirely to fund projects overseas. And wouldn't you know, just days later, God did, in fact, provide someone to underwrite Spoken! Our anonymous donor had only one request: that we make the event one that would glorify God. That was a pretty simple request.

The table was set for an incredible evening, and three weeks prior to the event, all 740 seats were sold out! As our Topeka-based team came together, our new venue had come alive. We knew that God had brought together the right team of volunteers and people attending that night, and we were going to leave the results up to Him. Our need was high, and it was obvious that God knew the need, and that He was planning something amazing!

In many cases, it is very difficult to ask for donations—but that night the vision and the need seemed easy to share, and the group that came together embraced it and eagerly joined our team. The whole evening went off without a hitch, and we raised over $300,000 for overseas projects. Our prayers had been answered. We could officially begin work in the Philippines.

All the local news stations and the newspaper came to report on the story. Even Kansas Governor Sam Brownback attended and would later tell us that he was 100% behind the TMP movement. The goal for the evening was to raise enough money in one night to bring true transformation to an entire community in the Philippines. The response of those in attendance gave us the opportunity to launch our mission in four Filipino trash dump communities!

Many times, it is easy to see God's hand at work overseas, but we all must embrace our role here in the States and realize that it is the same God who moves all over His creation. In His eyes, the person who donates their time and money here is just as important in His global mission as those who go. The Church' mission involves both going and sending. Without that partnership, His church is not complete.

GOOD WORD: INVESTING WISELY
~ DR. JIM CONGDON

There are a lot of dollar signs in this chapter. Why are missions organizations and missionaries always asking us for money? Is money the "life blood" of ministry?

Conference speaker, Michael Oh, shocked his listeners recently by saying, "Some pastors think their people value money too much. I disagree. I think people value their money too little. Money is like blood. There is great value and blessing in it. But money, like blood, is meant to flow. To flow through the body. To clean and cleanse and bless and enrich and support and give life... What a shame to miss out on the fullness of God's blessing in giving sacrificially and generously for the flow of blood and blessing to the whole body of Christ, to the global Body, for the global spread of the gospel."

Even if Scripture would shudder at Oh's elevating money to the level of blood (the life of the Body is certainly not money, see Leviticus 17:11), the Bible does agree that money is a bad master but a wonderful servant, which should be put it to work to serve God's world missions strategy "of calling out of every tribe and tongue and nation a chosen people for the praise of the glory of his grace" (John Piper).

Two comments:

1. We're not giving as we should.

Today there are two big problems with missions and money, one on the giving side—what you and I give; the other on the spending side—what missions do with what we give.

On the giving side, those of us who believe in the Gospel and evangelism are stingy. Fifty years ago, evangelicals gave 6% of their income to the church. As incomes have risen, our giving has dropped to just over 4%. And our evangelical churches no longer support world missions as they once did. Instead of giving at least 10% of their income to missions, the percentage has dropped to 2.1%. *(Source: http://www.christianitytoday.com/ct/2011/ february/howevangelicalsgive.html)*

So the first problem is stinginess or greed. But when God seizes your heart with His love for the lost, with His passion for His glory, and with the desire to lay up eternal treasure in heaven, nothing can stop you from investing hugely in leading people to life in Christ. To your delight, you will find that giving is the drain plug for greed.

2. Many missions and charities are spending our money unwisely.

The other problem is on the spending side. Recent studies have revealed that we have been hurting our own cause in the way we have tried to save the world. For example, Robert Lupton points out in Toxic Charity: How Churches and Charities Hurt Those They Help (And How to Reverse It), "When we do for those in need what they have the capacity to do for themselves we disempower them."

Instead of "I'm going to bless you" giving that creates dependency and saps dignity, we need to follow a hands-on partnership model. Trash Mountain Project is committed to this model in each community it serves. Instead of beginning with handouts, it begins by creating a mutually beneficial partnership with a local church or ministry. Then it empowers that local ministry to lift up the impoverished to spiritual life and economic health.

IF YOU WANT TO MAKE GOD LAUGH, TELL HIM YOUR PLANS

The Spoken event had become the catalyst for TMP returning to the Philippines. This time, we knew we needed to take the time to share the great news of what God had done in one evening through His people at Spoken with our new Filipino partners and begin long-term plans for the mission.

Jon and I invited Pastor Ed Rotz to go with us since he had met Dr. Patacsil at the Wesleyan General Conference. He had also shared how intrigued he was by what God had already done, and wanted to be a part of what He would do next. We planned to leave on December 9, 2012. We thought it would just be a planning trip, but I had forgotten a famous quote that I find both funny and true: If you want to make God laugh, tell Him your plans.

In preparation for our trip, Ed had requested details of our plan. I simply chuckled, and told him to just show up for the flight, strap on his seatbelt, and come along for the ride because we had no idea what was going to happen this time. It was really important for us to have another set of eyes, especially someone we trust who was not a part of our staff. Most importantly, having Ed, the Superintendent of the Kansas Wesleyan Church, travel to the other side of the planet to help us launch this new partnership and project was a big deal. He knew that the Wesleyan Church was quickly developing into a major overseas partner for our ministry, *and* that his presence would speak volumes to our new friends.

I find it almost comedic the times when something providential happens in the most unlikely time and place. Waiting for our departing flight in the Los Angeles International Airport, I received one last text message before boarding the plane. It was from our office, and they were notifying us that we had just received a very large donation that we did not expect. No one really knew who the donor was, only that they had come to the Spoken event just weeks before.

The crazy part was that we had just been discussing some significant long-term needs and prayed that the Lord would continue providing as He did at our recent fundraising event. It is cool when you tell someone else about something that you have been praying for, and at that very moment, you receive a text message answering that prayer on God's behalf.

We arrived in Manila late in the evening. Our first two days would be spent meeting with Pastor Stanley and Dr. Patacsil. We had talked about building a school near the dump, and they had gathered some information to share with us about starting a school in the Philippines. We brought preliminary blueprints drawn up by an architect in the States. We also planned to present our model of missions to them, further illustrating the available tools that we could bring into this partnership, and see what best fit with their vision for the community. This would give us a chance to discuss the order of steps needed to reach our collective goals for the Tanza 1 community project.

On the way to the community, our driver, also named Ed, whom we had never met, proceeded to tell his life story. He used to own a successful bakery in Manila. Since selling his business, he shared that he had a dream of teaching unemployed people the skill of baking bread to create a source of income. There is a type of bread that is very popular among Filipinos. It is simple to make and could easily be made in mass quantity.

Ed felt that it could be a great project for individuals or ministries to create income and become more self-sustaining long-term. He had no idea who we were and that this was just the type of training we could teach in our schools and kitchens. Such a project would not only feed the children attending the program, but also help provide the resources our partners would need for sustainability and growth.

As we listened to his story, we had the distinct feeling that God had put this man in our path for a reason. We told him what we do, and that we would love to join him in making his dream a reality in serving those in need within the community he was driving us to. His eyes lit up and a huge smile stretched across his face and he said, "I'm in!"

JESUS FEEDS 250

As the conversation with our driver was ending, Rick chimed in from the back seat that he needed to share what happened a few days earlier. He explained how his dad had organized a small pastor's training conference for four to five pastors in the San Mateo area. Rick had assisted his dad by raising some money to prepare a lunch for those in attendance and extra to feed at least 50 kids in the community who might show up to the event. Rick's mother is a school administrator, and the chef from her school offered to prepare the food for the event, a traditional dish called Pancit (noodles, vegetables, and chicken). She stretched the ingredients they purchased as far as she could and said the meal would feed around 70 people if they limited the portion size.

When they arrived at the site and set up the food for lunch, it appeared that over 200 kids had already caught wind of the free food and were waiting for their chance to eat. Their team didn't know what to do. They dreaded having to turn people away, but had no money or time to get more food. Even if they had the resources, they didn't have any way to go find the food this late in the process. They prayed over the food, thanked God for what He had provided, and began serving the food to those who had arrived the earliest.

As they began filling the plates with food, they noticed something very strange after serving roughly 100 people. They had already given food to more people than they had planned based on the amount of food that was prepared, and, mysteriously, there was still a gigantic pot of Pancit left! They kept serving 10 to 20 plates at a time and the food just kept coming. They all began to laugh and praise God as their only way of explaining this was that the food was miraculously multiplying.

The kids and all the other guests were served large portions and were full at the end of the meal. When they finished serving all the people there was enough to send food home with all the pastors for their families. After hearing this story, I questioned Rick about how he knew that they had served 250 people. He started laughing and told me that after the meal they were all discussing this phenomenon and wondered how many people they had actually served that day. It was then that he remembered the sealed package of plates that he had brought for the event. He went and found the plate package. It clearly said 250 paper plates, and it was completely empty! All we could say in response to that story was, "Wow, it sounds eerily like some stories we had read in the Bible." I guess if Jesus could multiply fish and bread 2,000 years ago, He can surely multiply Pancit today.

For me, this story had a deeper meaning that was screaming in my mind as Rick spoke. Just a few days before heading to Manila for that trip, David Yeazell, the man editing the book you are reading, had shared a story with me about a group that had traveled to Juarez, Mexico back in the 1980s with food to feed the people living in a trash dump community. They planned for a certain number and then fed two to three times more people, and had leftovers to send home with each person who attended.

David told me that when he had researched Trash Mountain Project's mission, one of the reasons he agreed to become our book editor was that the story he had read decades before about the group in Juarez had always stuck with him in a unique way. He had no way of knowing that, literally, the day he shared that story with me on the phone, a similar event was taking place in Manila with the group that he would soon be writing about. Go figure!

A 15-YEAR PRAYER ANSWERED

As we pulled up to Vista Wesleyan Church in the Tanza 1 trash dump community, we saw Dr. Alberto Patacsil and his wife, Dorcas, and Pastor Stanley Rabago and his wife, Noreen, coming to greet us. Sitting down to discuss the future of our partnership, I felt that it was important that I share with them what had happened on our first trip—how God had moved to bring us to the Philippines, and the unusual events that transpired once we were there.

After sharing the story of our first visit, we looked around the silent room at blank stares that turned into smiles, laughter, and then praise to Jesus. Stanley and Noreen were in tears as they explained how much of a confirmation this all was for them. They told us that they had been praying over 15 years that God would send His people to join them in their vision to build a school and develop their ministry to the community.

How are we supposed to process the concept of being used by God to be a small part of the answer to a 15-year prayer? Have you ever honestly prayed for something for 15 years? I could not think of a time that I had done such a thing, and then to have an opportunity like that to join in someone else's prayer. We couldn't help but think that everything we had witnessed and been a part of over the prior four years was leading to that moment. Leading to moments just like this one that will be the answer to a prayer that is being prayed right now in some other country that is not even on our radar. It reminds us how small we are; yet how important we all are to God and His plan.

Noreen went on to explain that she had always dreamed of someday becoming a Christian school principal, but that she needed to go back to school to finish her graduate degree to do so. We learned that she had a network of teachers she was friends with who had a similar dream to become a part of a school that would give them the opportunity to serve God and His children in need. It started becoming obvious to us that the first phase in the development of this community would be to build a school next to their church that could meet the educational, physical, spiritual, and emotional needs of the children in Tanza 1.

I explained that if we were to move forward with this partnership it was important that we be more of a silent partner that assisted them in every way we could. We requested that they not call it the Trash Mountain School. It was *their* vision and ministry, not ours. We wanted to join them by sharing what God had blessed us with: great people for project development who are businessmen and women, health care professionals, contractors, teachers, pastors and so many others who could lend a hand and provide the resources to invest in this important ministry work. We simply wanted to partner with them to get the school up and running and would develop the operations as long as needed while we all worked together to bring all of their outreach programs to a place of self-sustainability.

Our new Filipino partners immediately jumped into the conversation and began naming what they could do to reach self-sustainability: aquaponics, animal husbandry, a bakery, and technical school products. They understood the needs in other similar communities and knew that the sooner they could reach their goals, the sooner TMP could move on to other places of need. Not only this, but they wanted to be involved in the development of other Filipino trash dump communities, using the Tanza 1 community as a template to be replicated all over their country

I remember looking over at Pastor Ed as all of this was going down. He shot me a look of bewilderment that he would later explain was utter amazement at the team that God had brought together in that place for His purpose. He told me that if he could have scripted how the partnership might work, it wouldn't have worked out any better. He felt that the Holy Spirit's presence was so strong in this moment that it simply couldn't fail.

It is only in our human efforts that we fail. But, when we let go of our own plans and join ourselves to the plans of our Heavenly Father, we can expect success. Hearing those words from a man for whom I have the deepest respect and love for brought me to tears. I revisited a question I had asked him just seven months before after returning from our first trip to the Philippines, "Why us?" His reply was, "I don't know, Brett, but I think it can be summed up in one word...grace."

THE DREAM TEAM

Sitting down to lunch that afternoon, I mentioned to Dr. Patacsil that we wanted to visit some other trash dump communities throughout the Philippines. When I asked how much it would cost to take small plane trips to neighboring islands, he suggested something that caught us off guard. He had done some research since our earlier visit, and he said that he could take us to 20 dump communities in one week without ever leaving the island of Luzon. We simply had to follow the main highway. Excited about his offer, I quickly realized that his research illustrated that there were most likely well over 100 trash dump communities throughout the Philippine Islands, which meant that our previous estimate of 18 was just slightly low. Wow!

The next day Ed, Jon, and I arrived back out at the church in Tanza 1 and noticed some new faces among our friends. There were two engineers, an architect, and Dr. Patacsil's daughter who was finishing her Master's degree in Urban Development. We shared the plans with the engineers, and they were all on board to assist in any way they could. Two of them were new to the Faith and were amazed by the story of how everything had come together between TMP and Vista Wesleyan Church. As we talked, it become obvious that we had all been brought together with a much greater purpose that needed all of us to succeed.

Just before we broke for lunch, Dr. Patacsil asked if he could have everybody's attention as he had something he needed to share with us. He stood up and emotionally shared that this had been a very humbling process for him personally. He said that he needed to ask for our forgiveness about something. The room grew silent as this highly respected leader in the Church began to choke up. He said that he had asked God to forgive him for a sin of omission. He admitted that he had knowingly ignored the trash dump subculture of his country. He had always looked at the people that chose to live in garbage as being unreachable or even undeserving of his love. They were part of the trash and just seemed too dirty to love. That was wrong.

Seeing how God had brought all of us together, he knew that God cared about the very people he had ignored for so long. God had called us to be a light of hope in a hopeless place, and that it didn't get much more hopeless than a community of people living, working, and dying in trash. He said that in his ignorance he had ignored the most hopeless and despicable people in his country, but that would stop today.

He went on saying that he knew this was one community, and his research had estimated there were roughly 100 such communities in the country. He said that what we did in Tanza 1 would no doubt be a model of missions to be replicated in other areas throughout the country. Whether it happened by planting churches or working with other churches outside of the

Wesleyan denomination didn't matter—they would work with whoever had a similar vision to meet the needs of the people God had called them to serve. The selfless leadership of this man of God humbled us all.

THE STORY HAD NOT ENDED

After leaving Tanza 1, we went to San Mateo, pulled up to the church and saw Pastor Joemar and Don Don. It was a celebration among friends. Just as we did the day before, we shared what had transpired on the previous trip, and they were equally as amazed at God's movement—and the story we all found ourselves in that only He could author. They began sharing their hearts and vision for the San Mateo dump community, and how they felt called to partner together with us as we share the Gospel and Christ's love with the lost.

Knowing that we were considering the possibility of simultaneously beginning ministry work in Tanza 1 and San Mateo, we asked Pastor Joemar what his plans were and how his family was doing. He was modest about telling us that his family went without food and basic necessities on a regular basis to maintain his position as a pastor in the San Mateo dump community. He went on to tell us that he had just turned down a job—driving a taxi that would have him working 29 out of 30 days a month. It would have met his family's needs, but taken him away from his call as pastor to his community. He knew he was to continue being the pastor of the church, but because it paid him nothing. He was not sure how he would care for his family. It was emotional hearing him speak, and I can tell you that I had never felt more thankful, yet humbled by a man that was literally putting it all on the line for Jesus.

A similar scenario unfolded as we had seen in Tanza 1 the day before as we all agreed that God had brought this incredible team of people together to carry out His vision for that community. We decided to pledge our support for Joemar and his family as a first step in moving forward with the San Mateo mission. And we all agreed that this was just the beginning of a much bigger story that was yet to be written. He requested that we thank all of the generous supporters of our ministry that made it all possible. What a picture of how all the gifts of God's Spirit work together for His glory.

And as we were about to leave, Jon turned to Joemar and asked if we could go visit Eugene, the little boy we had prayed over several months before. And at that moment, Don Don shot me a look that I will never forget. It was a mysterious look that would soon make perfect sense.

Chapter 17:

THE MIRACLE CONTINUES

———◆◆◆———

As we began the walk from the San Mateo church towards the community we had spent the night in just seven short months prior, I shared with Joemar and Don Don how much it meant to Jon, Fran, and me that they stayed up all night with us. I said, "You had no idea of my past experience in a similar situation when I almost died. But God knew my feeble fears, and sent you as our protectors. Why did you do that?" They smiled and then Don Don responded with a very serious look on his face and said, "I was willing to give my life to protect the three of you, because I knew that God had sent you. I would do whatever it took to protect you even to the point of death. And because of this, I knew that God would not abandon me just as he didn't abandon David when he defeated Goliath."

The flood of emotion and thoughts that filled my mind at that moment is difficult to put into words. God had rescued us in Cambodia by sending His guardian angels to protect us—and, through Joemar and Don Don, He sent His living saints to protect in the same way. I do not take such experiences for granted. I rest in the fact that God protects His children. But at the same time, I know that His protection does not always mean physically making it through what He has asked of us. In the Bible He protected His own disciples, yet at least 11 out of the 12 apostles died at the hands of their enemies.

A MYSTERIOUS REVELATION

As we reached the community where we had stayed the night, we recognized many familiar faces, including the elderly man who had welcomed us as his family's guests. We were excited to see them again, and, as they greeted us, Jon asked where Eugene was. They explained that Eugene, his parents, and his aunt had to move because they were no longer able to sustain their family as the price of metal recyclables had dropped from five pesos per kilo to one peso. The family had moved to a small fishing village on an island in the middle of Laguna De Bay, a large lake south of Manila. Eugene's father had been given a job on the island, and it was providing their family with much-needed income.

Jon began questioning Eugene's brother-in-law, who was still living in San Mateo, to see if we could get any kind of update on Eugene's legs. His response sent shivers up my spine. He said, "Eugene's legs are fine now, and he is even playing basketball with his friends." I glanced at Jon and Ed with a look that said, *Did you guys just hear what I heard?*

At times, we had misinterpreted information due to translation issues. With something this important, we couldn't just assume we heard him clearly, so we pressed him to clarify what he had just said. We questioned whether Eugene had received any further medical attention or had been given some kind of braces for his legs. We knew that this was a long shot. Dr. Sabado had evaluated him on our first trip and said that there was nothing that could be done for him due to the permanent damage to his legs from the surgery he had undergone as a an 11-month-old baby.

His mother had told us that he had a bacterial infection that had destroyed his muscle tissue. The only way to spare his life was to remove all of the infected tissue from his legs. On our prior visit, I recall seeing the large surgical scars and missing tissue down to the bone from the surgery.

Eugene's brother-in-law continued, telling us that they had rubbed aloe on Eugene's legs and that was the only medical attention he had received since we had seen him in May. Of course we knew that it would take some rather potent aloe to make a boy walk when he had never done so in his life. During our conversation, Jon and I were thrown back to the depression we felt a half a year prior when the three of us prayed over Eugene and did not see him healed. Could it really be that he was in fact healed?

Eugene's brother-in-law knew where Eugene lived, and we asked him to take us to him. We knew we couldn't report this unbelievable story until we had real confirmation of what we had just heard. Too many times, false information is reported in God's name, and all it does is drag His name through the mud and make His people look foolish. We wanted neither to happen on our watch. We all wanted to go and see Eugene and get the whole story and see whether God had, in fact, healed this young boy. As we spoke, Jon's demeanor was very adamant about finding Eugene and confirming the story.

The excitement in the car as we pulled away was almost palpable. As we returned to the house, Jon jumped out of the car and ran up to our room. When I walked in, I noticed that he was rifling through his bag, apparently looking for something. He stopped and read something for a few moments, and then he turned and handed me his journal entry from the day we returned from staying the night out at San Mateo on our previous trip. Here is what I read:

Before leaving the community, we extend our thanks and love to them. We tell them we will return, and they are looking forward to it. We meet a young kid named Eugene before leaving. He cannot walk because of an illness he had a while back. Earlier that day, I saw his mother massaging his legs as he stayed in his wood hut, and the other children played and laughed. We approached him and he began to cry. His mother holds him and we extend friendly smiles and encouragement. Fran, our doctor tries to console him, and he begins to settle down. We gather around and pray for him, each believing for a full healing. I cry as I think about a child like this who probably cannot dream and think of a bright future in the situation he is in. I ask God why? Why Eugene, how come that is not me sitting there. What do we not see that God does? Maybe sometimes it is my lack of understanding or something, but I question why we see so much hurt in these kids? They endure so much and in so many instances, NO ONE is helping. We are such blessed people, yet we do nothing about the hurt around the world. I include myself in this, we have to do more. Though we all believed, Eugene was not miraculously healed, he will one day though. I believe that. I will see Eugene walk.

After I finished reading it, Jon looked at me with tears in his eyes and said, "We need to find Eugene." What could I say? I wanted to find Eugene before reading the journal, but this passage made it an absolute must before we returned home.

THE FAITH OF A CHILD

We made the decision to go visit Eugene's island on Sunday but knew that first we needed to follow up with Marivic at the Payatas trash dump community. Arriving at her ministry, we walked into a room full of children singing and worshiping. Marivic approached us with a very serious look on her face and pulled us aside to introduce us to Mary Loi, a nine-year-old girl she had e-mailed us about.

We learned that Mary Loi had a history of fluid buildup in a cavity behind her ears that had been bleeding for most of her life. It was very painful and had caused extensive damage to her hearing and to her quality of life.

Our first response was to ask if there was anything that could be done and whether she had visited doctors concerning her condition. Marivic and Mary Loi's mother informed us that there was a surgery that could be done for around $1,000, but that they could not afford to pay for the operation.

Mary Loi was very shy. but we were able to talk with her and asked her if we could pray for her. She immediately said, "Yes." Before we began the prayer, we asked if she believed in Jesus Christ. She said, "Yes." We continued and asked her if she believed that He could heal her. Her response was something so deeply biblical that it floored us all. She didn't say that she wanted Jesus to heal her of her ailment. Instead she said, "I just want to be closer to Jesus."

Those eight simple words said it all. Wow! And from a child that had pretty much been in pain her entire life. I personally can't complain to God and others enough when I have a simple head cold. And this child had dealt with a lifelong ailment and only wanted to be closer to Jesus. Oh what we can learn from the faith of a child.

We spent a very intense moment in prayer with Mary Loi, fully believing God would heal her. Not because we had any kind of power in ourselves, other than the power of God that we were calling on. And honestly, with the faith that Jesus must have seen in His young daughter, shouldn't we have expected the miraculous?

In addition to the faithful prayer that we shared together, I began having flashbacks to a conversation I had with Michael Barrett in Cambodia over three years before. We had decided then that we didn't want to pray a prayer we were not willing to be the answer to. So we made the decision to move forward and provide the resources for whatever treatment Mary Loi needed in her recovery.

I think it is naïve to believe that all situations like Mary Loi's should require the power of God's healing intervention. If there are medical procedures that can heal someone in need, and He has given us the financial resources to provide such a service, isn't that the same thing? God's providence is God's providence. And if He has provided the tools to love and care for someone in need, isn't that an answer to the very prayer we just prayed?

Since that visit, we have learned that Mary Loi is doing much better, and we have been blessed to be in contact with an excellent ENT doctor that is willing to help...go God! But, in addition to that, God moved in another way in Mary Loi's life. A way that even doctors couldn't explain. But that will have to wait for another book at a future time—sorry!

JESUS TEACHES FROM A BOAT...AGAIN

Sunday morning, our final day in the Philippines, we went to church. We had Rick go to San Mateo to pick up those going with us to see Eugene. We had a limited window of time to visit him, so right after church we headed out on the two-hour journey. Arriving at the shore of Laguna De Bay, we learned that there would be a 30-minute boat ride to the island where Eugene's family lived.

Pastor Joemar and Don Don brought Eugene's sister and brother-in-law along to help us locate the family. Joemar and Don Don were also very excited to see him, as they had seen that Eugene had started to improve at some level before they moved and they wanted to see if he had been fully healed.

When we arrived at the coastal area of the lake it looked like an ocean because it is so big. We chartered one of the numerous boats taxiing out to different destinations on the lake.

As we pulled out into the lake, our entire group was very quiet. I drifted off into prayer, trying to prepare myself for what we might see in the coming moments. All of a sudden, it was like I saw tracers—like after looking into a light and then shutting your eyes—but it was not a group of dots or simple circles, it was a message..."Matthew 11." It was as clear as if I had written it down on paper. As it flashed across my closed eyes, I was startled and opened them, still seeing the remnant of Matthew 11.

I had never had an experience quite like that before. I looked over at Ed and Jon with what must have been a surprised expression. I asked if Jon could pull up Matthew 11 on his phone as I had not brought my Bible with me. I asked him to read the passage aloud so that we could all hear it together. The response all three of us had upon hearing that seemingly random biblical text was affected by a discussion we had over dinner the night prior. We had been discussing some fun theological mind benders including the question if John the Baptist was literally Elijah reborn. Was he the undead reappearing of Elijah hundreds of years after leaving earth?"

Ed and Jon admitted that they had never really pondered that question before. I am guessing that the topic was something fresh in my mind because after the Transfiguration, in Matthew 17, Jesus told the disciples that Elijah had already returned as John the Baptist. The only reason I remembered that passage so clearly was because of the Matthew 17 experience I had at San Mateo on our previous trip to the Philippines, which ended up leading us to Eugene and our eventual prayer for his healing.

That said, please believe me when I say that I am not the sharpest tool in the shed when it comes to scripture memorization. And, it's not because I don't see the deep value in it, I am just not very good at it. Furthermore, this might explain why God has chosen to reveal to me certain passages of His Word at just the right moment along the journey, guiding my steps and the movement of TMP. The Bible is to guide us. It was given to God's people to aid in the building of His kingdom, and we must hold strong to the words held within its pages.

Fast forward to the boat. As Jon began reading aloud the message held in Matthew 11, we were at once brought back to our conversation the night before when in just two verses we heard John the Baptist's name spoken. This caught our attention, but three verses later we were brought to tears as verse five hit our ears. It says, "The blind receive their sight and the LAME WALK, lepers are cleansed and the deaf hear, and the dead are raised up, and the poor have good news preached to them."

The words "deaf will hear" brought a flashback of the deaf woman at church in Florida that heard just long enough to receive a message from God to encourage us as we visited our first trash dump community in Honduras. She could never have known that four years later God would prompt me to read those words. And we were only minutes away from investigating the possibility of a child that had been lame his entire life being set free by that very same power of God.

And then it came, in verses 7 to 19, Jesus launches into His most extensive teaching on record concerning the identity of John the Baptist. In verse 14, He tells His disciples, "and if you are willing to accept it, he is Elijah who is to come."

Though we were all experiencing a bit of shock at what we were hearing, there was something very reassuring within the context of the message that was coming from this chapter in

Matthew. John the Baptist was seeking an answer about whether Jesus was, in fact, the Messiah that was to come. This was the man that Jesus made this statement about in verse 11: "Truly, I say to you, among those born of women there has arisen no one greater than John the Baptist." Even after hearing about all of the miracles that Jesus was performing, how could this prophet among prophets question whether He was, in fact, the Son of God?

That was reassuring to me because I am no prophet. I am a sinful man struggling to follow Christ in a way that glorifies His Father. And I feel that I have failed Him when I experience lapses of faith in whether God would really speak to me. Or whether we should spend the night out at San Mateo due to a fear of what could happen to us. Or whether we would miss a God-ordained meeting with the leader of the Filipino Wesleyan Church. And now, whether I really believed that a young boy who had never once stood on his own two feet could really be a walking miracle. God forgive me.

Jon then came to the final two verses, and read: "Take my yoke upon you, and learn from me, for I am gentle and lowly in heart, and you will find rest for your souls. For my yoke is easy, and my burden is light." These words brought peace to the three of us. We were at a place of trust in God no matter what we found on the island. Whether Eugene was healed or not, we knew God was in control. We were simply passengers on a journey that He was leading.

THE LAME WILL WALK

Our boat guide soon informed us that we would be pulling up to the island. The anticipation was absolutely killing us! As we came around the final bend, we saw the island with a hillside covered by 40 to 50 small lean-to-style homes. There were people scattered throughout the community, many huddled around campfires. As we pulled into the dock, we noticed two kids playing basketball on a dirt court with an improvised hoop.

Eugene's brother-in-law told us that he was now able to play basketball, but those boys seemed too big to be Eugene.

Then, Eugene's sister came to the front of the boat and pointed towards a small boy swimming near the beach and said, "Eugene." Instantly, Jon jumped to the front edge of the boat to get a better look and nearly fell into the water, camera in hand. Eugene's family obviously knew it was him, and were clearly excited to see him. The boy they were pointing at dove under the water and when he resurfaced Jon screamed, "That's Eugene!"

But, this had to be a different child. The first time we met him, we were unable to approach him without him screaming and crying. But the boy we were watching now was smiling ear to ear as he bobbed up and down in the water. Not to mention the fact that he was swimming! How could he swim if his legs were not working? Dumbfounded, we all stared as he reached the shore and jumped out of the water and then proceeded to sprint up the hill in front of him. We could hardly believe what we were seeing.

At land, we jumped off the boat and quickly followed the path Eugene had taken up the hill, still not 100% sure it was him. Call us skeptics...so pathetic. As we approached the top of the hill, we recognized Eugene's mother, Manicia, and aunt sitting outside of the home he had run to. It was obvious that they recognized us, as his mom greeted us with an excited smile and a hug. As Rick translated our questions to her, I simply couldn't get over the fact that I was watching Eugene climb the tree next to us.

Remembering what Dr. Sabado had informed us of prior to praying for Eugene, we wanted to be 100% sure that we had not misunderstood anything about his condition. We grilled Manicia with questions for about 15 minutes. We asked her if we had been mistaken about his condition. Maybe he had just been recently hurt when we saw him. Had he really been lame for his entire childhood? She calmly explained again how he had gotten very sick with an infection that spread throughout his legs when he was 11-months-old, and due to the infection he had undergone emergency surgery to remove all of the infected tissue in his legs. And she confirmed that he had never walked. Ever.

When Manicia reassured us that Eugene had undergone no medical treatment since the last time we had seen him we asked what she thought had happened to him. She began choking up as she mustered up the words, "Jesus healed him." She pointed at Jon and me and said, "I remember them as well as their Filipino doctor friend that stayed the night in our community. They prayed for my son in Jesus' name, and he was healed." She went on to say, "I am a woman of faith, and I had prayed every day since his surgery that Jesus would heal him. Being a mother, it was very difficult watching my son in such pain. For seven years, multiple times every day I massaged his legs to bring him some comfort and relief. I had to console him as he watched all of the other kids playing. I did my best to reassure him that God still loved him and had a plan for his life. But, there was no relief. Not until a few days after you joined me in praying for my son. Something happened."

She described how within just a few days after our prayer he began to prop himself up. He then tried to take small steps. And all of a sudden he was walking, then running, jumping, and even playing basketball with the other kids! She continued, "Since we moved to this island, he has been sick a few times with fever, but his legs are 100% healed!" We knew that Jesus had healed Eugene, and he knew it too.

Manicia called her son over so that we could see his legs. She pointed at the scars and described how the previous gaps of missing muscle tissue looked nothing like they had before. The tissue had physically grown back in a matter of a few short weeks. Jon, Fran, and I confirmed with each other that we had also seen the gaps. For Fran, that was what was most devastating about Eugene's condition. He had told us that there were no surgical options that he knew of that could replace removed tissue. Jon and I stared in amazement at the scars on otherwise normal and functioning legs.

As we talked to Manicia, a large group of people from their new community had gathered around and were listening to us and watching what was happening. They had never had Americans in their community, and it was causing a small commotion. I asked Manicia if there was a church on the island, or if anyone there was a follower of Jesus. She replied, "No, only my family." Jon, Ed and I looked at each other with smiles on our faces. We turned to Pastor Joemar and said, "Run with it, brother. You have a group of people who just heard about this boy who was healed, and they have no idea how something like that could happen. It's time you explain it to them."

Being that it was December, Joemar decided to preach a Christmas/Gospel message to all who were willing to listen. At the end of his message, he asked the group if they wanted to know the Jesus who had healed Eugene? Every single person that was standing there made a commitment to follow Jesus Christ! And since they had not previously heard of Jesus, I asked if they knew what a Bible was. They responded, "No, what's that?" We explained that it is a book written by God that contains the story of Jesus, the One they had just committed to following. With smiles on their faces, they asked, "Could you bring those to us?"

Conclusion:

HOW DOES IT END?

————•◦•————

"And Jesus came and said to them, 'All authority in heaven and on earth has been given to me. Go therefore and make disciples of all nations, baptizing them in the name of the Father and of the Son and of the Holy Spirit, teaching them to observe all that I have commanded you. And behold, I am with you always, to the end of the age.'" (Matthew 28:18-20)

As we look back on the final event of this book, it appears to be so much more than the miraculous healing of one of God's children. The fact that a child who had suffered for seven years was healed is amazing, and would obviously be enough to bring joy not only to him and his family but to all of us.

But could it be possible that God would take something that brought so much pain and suffering to this family, and use it for the good of His kingdom? We believe that that is exactly what happened.

If you look at the miracles throughout the Bible, they were all initiated to continue the story of God's redemption for His creation. Miracles don't occur for show, no matter what some "faith healers" would lead us to believe. We believe that miracles occur when they are connected to the carrying out of the Great Commission of Jesus Christ.

And that is exactly what happened with Eugene and his family. God was fully aware that they were going to be forced to move from the San Mateo trash dump community to an island that was inhabited by children that He planned to draw into His family.

And to do this, He chose to perform a miracle on a little boy whose mother had been praying for him for seven years. God chose to draw us in to the story to be a part of that moment we had just experienced together. And, God used him and his suffering to bring the Gospel to a completely unreached group of people.

When we got back on the boat to leave the island and return home, Jon showed me the video he had taken of Eugene. He was looking back over his shoulder at the camera with a huge smile on his face. He had the exact same expression that we had seen on Jeni's face over a year before. Same position, same look over the shoulder, and same smile. When you see them side-by-side, you see JOY. And one child being healed led us to an entirely different country, and resulted in several new TMP location births...and to another young child being healed of an incurable ailment. Only God could accomplish such a miraculous thing!

TO BE CONTINUED...

Brett and I have chosen to end this book without a big bang or an emotional climax. There's no period at the end of this book. Instead, it's ending with an ellipsis (...), like the end of the movie with a sequel to be released at a future date. If you've seen a *Hobbit*, or *Hunger Games* flick lately, you get the picture.

In other words, this book ends like the Book of Acts ends. The ending of the book of Acts disappoints many readers of the Bible. The rest of the book is so exciting: tongues of fire, prison escapes, and liars falling dead, a Jewish assassin converted to Christian evangelist, magic, miracles, shipwreck, and snakebite. And then this ho-hum ending: "He lived there two whole years at his own expense and welcomed all who came to him, proclaiming the kingdom of God and teaching about the Lord Jesus Christ with all boldness and without hindrance" (Acts 28:30-31).

That's it? That's a progress report, not an ending! So why does Luke end his Book Two (The Book of Luke is Book One) this way? Because like *The Lord of the Rings,* and *Hunger Games,* this is a trilogy, that's why! The story is not complete. Paul had arrived in Rome, but Jesus had predicted that "my witnesses" will go to "the uttermost parts of the earth" (Acts 1:8), so there's lots more to come before the story ends.

In other words, Luke is ending with "to be continued." He is alerting us that the end of Acts is not the end of the story. There's a Book Three coming. Not one that he would write, but one that the Holy Spirit would write in the outreach of the Church, with future Christians playing key roles.

In this epic movie trilogy, you and I are cast as actors in the final movie! And the implied question to you and me in the Book of Acts is: How will you continue the story?

Like the Book of Acts, this book ends with a non-ending. That's because the Trash Mountain story is "to be continued." This is not about one story or one person—it is about the ongoing story of God's providence in this world and in His mission.

Those of us watching God use TMP know that this ministry is young, on the rise, growing, and spreading. As we read the final chapter, we ask "what's coming next?" Trash Mountain Project doesn't know. I, Jim, don't have a clue. Brett, and the TMP team don't know. Only God knows. But the invitation is out there. Would you like to be an actor in the sequel? Would you like to be part of the next book? Would you like to help write the rest of the story? Then join the team, and be a part of the story that continues this conclusion...

INDEX OF PHOTOGRAPHS

About the Authors

BRETT DURBIN

B rett Durbin jumped on a plane to Honduras in search of a worthy cause to bring back to his church, and what he found changed his life. A college pastor for over two years in Lakeland, Florida, Brett holds Bachelor's and Master's degrees in Criminal Justice and a Master of Arts in Christian Leadership from Asbury Theological Seminary. In addition to his duties with Trash Mountain Project, Brett is an adjunct professor at Southeastern University teaching criminal justice and theology. He would love to eavesdrop on a conversation between C.S. Lewis, Mother Teresa, and Francis Chan, but understands that this dream will have to wait for another time and place.

One of Brett's life goals is to always be as transparent as possible and to always strive to love Christ through protecting and serving His children. All things are possible for the Creator of all things. He is married to the most incredible person on the face of the planet, Jaelle, and is blessed to be the father of five: Gabriel, Matthew, Susan, Josiah and Jeremiah. Brett thanks God every day that He has given him the opportunity to be a part of this incredible organization. Brett's motivation is Him, and to serve the least, the lost, and the forgotten.

"I have always searched for the true meaning of discipleship... and I found it on a mountain of trash." (Brett Durbin)

DR. JIM CONGDON

Jim has served as the Senior Pastor of Topeka Bible Church in Kansas for 30 years. During his tenure the church has grown to over 1,400 in attendance. Jim received a Bachelor of Science (B.S.) in Mathematics from Wheaton College (1971); Certificate in Bible from Multnomah School of the Bible (1972); Master of Theology (Th.M.) in Old Testament Hebrew from Dallas Theological Seminary—winner of the Old Testament Award (1976); Doctor of Ministry (D. Min.) from Evangelical Divinity School in Illinois (1996).

Jim and his wife, Melody, have been married since 1978 and have four children: Adriel (Daniel), Mark (Katy), Doug (Leigh), and Craig (Emily); and four perfect grandchildren, Liviya, Judah, Cora, and Asher.

Jim's favorite hobbies include playing volleyball and basketball, studying the Bible, leading tours to the lands of the Bible, doing archaeological digs, strategizing about outreach to Jews and to the nation of India, teaching Wisdom Literature at a local high school, reading, playing piano, traveling with Melody, collecting ancient pottery, spending time with his children and grandchildren, and talking to people about Christ.

ABOUT TRASH MOUNTAIN PROJECT

O n behalf of the entire Trash Mountain Tribe, we'd like to thank you for reading our first book outlining the story of Trash Mountain Project. Many times throughout the Bible we find that God makes mention of "waste places". Encouragingly, in many such passages in Scripture, there is a promise from God concerning the waste places throughout the world. He promises to comfort and rebuild such places so that these forgotten people will know that He is the Lord and that He loves and cares for them even in the darkest corners of His creation (Isaiah 51:3, Ezekiel 36:10-11). Our hope is that God continues to use this ministry to rebuild and shine His light of love on the waste places around the world.

We at Trash Mountain Project believe that all of us have been called to love, serve, protect, and provide for the needs of our discarded neighbors around the world. It is our mission to live out Christ's command to care for orphans, widows, the poor, criminal, hopeless, and forgotten. We invite you to partner with us in an effort to love and provide for those whom everyone but God has abandoned.

Our organization is focused entirely on following the commands of Jesus Christ. He is not only the central figure in the greatest story to have ever unfolded within our world, but He Himself was a great storyteller throughout His ministry. He communicated with the world through story, and we believe he is still doing so today. The book you have just completed is just one small segment of His ongoing story around the world, and we hope that it has encouraged and blessed you in your pursuit of God.

If you would like more information about how to become a part of the Trash Mountain Project story, please go to our website at **www.trashmountain.com** or call our U.S. headquarters at **785-246-6845**.